GOD
the
SAVIOR

*Our Freedom in Christ and Our Role
in the Restoration of All Things*

STUDY GUIDE I EIGHT SESSIONS

RANDY FRAZEE

Harper*Christian*
Resources

CONTENTS

HOW TO USE THIS GUIDE

SCOPE AND SEQUENCE

The story of the Bible reveals that heaven and earth are woven more closely together than we might think. All through the Bible, we find two parallel and beautiful dramas unfolding.

There is the **lower story**. Humans live on earth and see things from a horizontal perspective. We can't see what is around the bend but must make decisions on which way to go, where we will live, and how we will respond to what happens to us. We focus on getting through the day as best we can. We interpret why we think other people do what they do. We struggle to know why certain things happen and why other things don't happen.

Then there is the **upper story**. This is how the story is unfolding from God's perspective. Heaven is breaking into our world, and the story of God's seeking love, perpetual grace, and longing for a relationship with ordinary people is breathtaking. Of course, as humans living on this earth, we won't always be able see what is taking place in this upper story. But we can be sure that God is always present, at work, and active in every detail of our lives.

The objective of *God the Savior*—the third in a series of three small-group studies in *The Story* series—is to introduce you to these lower and upper stories. In this study, you will witness how all the Old Testament prophecies concerning the Messiah came to fulfillment in Jesus, the Son of God. You will examine how the early church was born after Jesus' ascension and how the disciples first spread the gospel. You will see how Paul continued to spread that gospel message through his missionary journeys in spite of persecution, hardships, and imprisonment. Finally, you will at look the vision that John received concerning Jesus' second coming and the end of time.

God wants to be with you. He wants to fill your life with greater purpose, meaning, and understanding. He wants to weave your lower story into his greater upper story that he has been writing. He wants to walk with you in every situation of life. As you recognize how closely his story and your story fit together, you *will* experience his love, grace, and wisdom.

SESSION OUTLINE

Each session is divided into two parts. In the group section, you will watch a video teaching from Randy Frazee and follow along with the outline that has been provided. (Note that you can watch these videos via streaming access at any time by following the instructions found on the inside front cover of this guide.) You will then recite the key verse(s), the key idea, and engage in some guided group discussion through the questions provided. You will close your group with a brief time of prayer.

PERSONAL STUDY

At the end of the group section, you will find a series of readings and study questions for you to go through on your own during the week. The first section will help you *know the story* by asking you to read several key passages from the Bible that were covered during your group time. The next section will help you *understand the story* through a short reading from Randy Frazee that will help you grasp the main takeaways. The third section will help you *live the story* by challenging you to put what you have learned into practice. The final section will help you *tell the story* through a short prompt for a conversation starter around a meal or dinner table. **The personal study is a critical component in helping you grasp the overall story of the Bible, so be sure to complete this study during the week before your next group meeting.**

GROUP SIZE

God the Savior can be experienced in a group setting (such as a Bible study, Sunday school class, or small-group gathering) and also as an individual study. If you are doing the study as a group with a large number of participants, it is recommended that everyone watches the video together and then breaks up into smaller groups of four to six for the discussion time. In either case, you can access the teaching videos via the streaming code found on the inside front cover.

MATERIALS NEEDED

Each participant in the group should have his or her own study guide. Although the course can be fully experienced with just the video and study guide, participants are also encouraged to have a copy of *The Story*, which includes selections from the *New International Version* that relate to each week's session.

Reading *The Story* as you go through the study will provide even deeper insights and make the journey even richer and more meaningful.

FACILITATION

Each group should appoint a facilitator who is responsible for keeping track of time during discussions and activities. Facilitators may also read questions aloud and monitor discussions, prompting participants to respond and ensuring everyone that has the opportunity to participate. (For more thorough instructions, refer to the the leader's guide that is included at the back of this guide.)

TIMELINE OF *THE STORY*

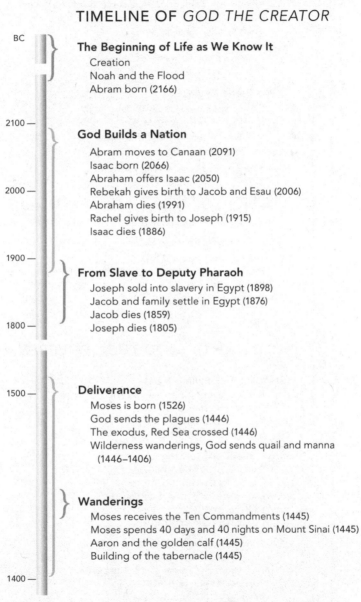

TIMELINE OF *GOD THE CREATOR*

BC

The Beginning of Life as We Know It
Creation
Noah and the Flood
Abram born (2166)

2100 —

God Builds a Nation
Abram moves to Canaan (2091)
Isaac born (2066)
Abraham offers Isaac (2050)
Rebekah gives birth to Jacob and Esau (2006)
Abraham dies (1991)
Rachel gives birth to Joseph (1915)
Isaac dies (1886)

2000 —

1900 —

From Slave to Deputy Pharaoh
Joseph sold into slavery in Egypt (1898)
Jacob and family settle in Egypt (1876)
Jacob dies (1859)
Joseph dies (1805)

1800 —

1500 —

Deliverance
Moses is born (1526)
God sends the plagues (1446)
The exodus, Red Sea crossed (1446)
Wilderness wanderings, God sends quail and manna
(1446–1406)

Wanderings
Moses receives the Ten Commandments (1445)
Moses spends 40 days and 40 nights on Mount Sinai (1445)
Aaron and the golden calf (1445)
Building of the tabernacle (1445)

1400 —

Note: Dates are approximate and dependent on the interpretative theories of various scholars.

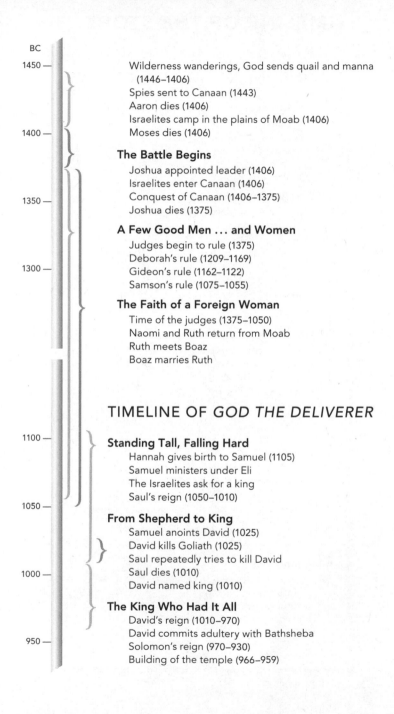

BC

1450 —
Wilderness wanderings, God sends quail and manna
(1446–1406)
Spies sent to Canaan (1443)
Aaron dies (1406)
Israelites camp in the plains of Moab (1406)

1400 —
Moses dies (1406)

The Battle Begins
Joshua appointed leader (1406)
Israelites enter Canaan (1406)
Conquest of Canaan (1406–1375)

1350 —
Joshua dies (1375)

A Few Good Men ... and Women
Judges begin to rule (1375)
Deborah's rule (1209–1169)

1300 —
Gideon's rule (1162–1122)
Samson's rule (1075–1055)

The Faith of a Foreign Woman
Time of the judges (1375–1050)
Naomi and Ruth return from Moab
Ruth meets Boaz
Boaz marries Ruth

TIMELINE OF *GOD THE DELIVERER*

1100 —
Standing Tall, Falling Hard
Hannah gives birth to Samuel (1105)
Samuel ministers under Eli
The Israelites ask for a king
Saul's reign (1050–1010)

1050 —
From Shepherd to King
Samuel anoints David (1025)
David kills Goliath (1025)
Saul repeatedly tries to kill David

1000 —
Saul dies (1010)
David named king (1010)

The King Who Had It All
David's reign (1010–970)
David commits adultery with Bathsheba
Solomon's reign (970–930)

950 —
Building of the temple (966–959)

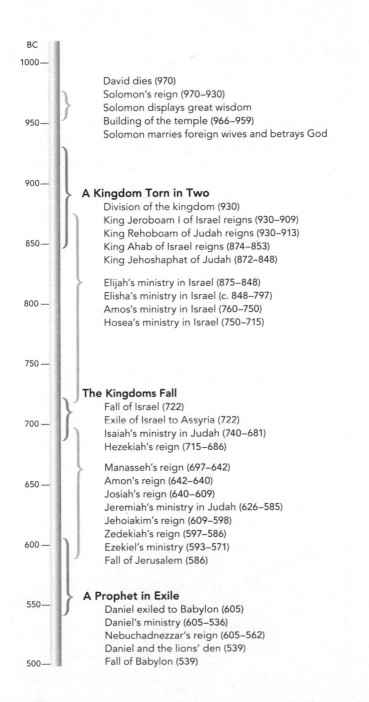

BC

1000 —

David dies (970)
Solomon's reign (970–930)
Solomon displays great wisdom
950 — Building of the temple (966–959)
Solomon marries foreign wives and betrays God

900 —

A Kingdom Torn in Two

Division of the kingdom (930)
King Jeroboam I of Israel reigns (930–909)
King Rehoboam of Judah reigns (930–913)
850 — King Ahab of Israel reigns (874–853)
King Jehoshaphat of Judah (872–848)

Elijah's ministry in Israel (875–848)
Elisha's ministry in Israel (c. 848–797)
800 — Amos's ministry in Israel (760–750)
Hosea's ministry in Israel (750–715)

750 —

The Kingdoms Fall

Fall of Israel (722)
Exile of Israel to Assyria (722)
700 — Isaiah's ministry in Judah (740–681)
Hezekiah's reign (715–686)

Manasseh's reign (697–642)
Amon's reign (642–640)
650 — Josiah's reign (640–609)
Jeremiah's ministry in Judah (626–585)
Jehoiakim's reign (609–598)
Zedekiah's reign (597–586)
600 — Ezekiel's ministry (593–571)
Fall of Jerusalem (586)

A Prophet in Exile

Daniel exiled to Babylon (605)
550 — Daniel's ministry (605–536)
Nebuchadnezzar's reign (605–562)
Daniel and the lions' den (539)
500 — Fall of Babylon (539)

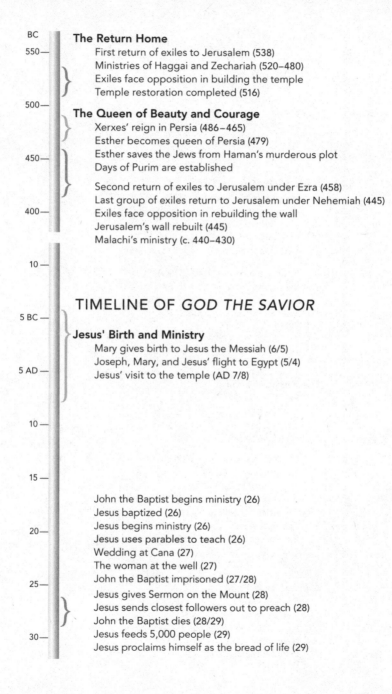

BC
550—

The Return Home
First return of exiles to Jerusalem (538)
Ministries of Haggai and Zechariah (520–480)
Exiles face opposition in building the temple
Temple restoration completed (516)

500—

The Queen of Beauty and Courage
Xerxes' reign in Persia (486–465)
Esther becomes queen of Persia (479)

450—
Esther saves the Jews from Haman's murderous plot
Days of Purim are established

Second return of exiles to Jerusalem under Ezra (458)
Last group of exiles return to Jerusalem under Nehemiah (445)

400—
Exiles face opposition in rebuilding the wall
Jerusalem's wall rebuilt (445)
Malachi's ministry (c. 440–430)

10—

TIMELINE OF *GOD THE SAVIOR*

5 BC—

Jesus' Birth and Ministry
Mary gives birth to Jesus the Messiah (6/5)
Joseph, Mary, and Jesus' flight to Egypt (5/4)

5 AD—
Jesus' visit to the temple (AD 7/8)

10—

15—

John the Baptist begins ministry (26)
Jesus baptized (26)

20—
Jesus begins ministry (26)
Jesus uses parables to teach (26)
Wedding at Cana (27)
The woman at the well (27)
John the Baptist imprisoned (27/28)

25—
Jesus gives Sermon on the Mount (28)
Jesus sends closest followers out to preach (28)
John the Baptist dies (28/29)

30—
Jesus feeds 5,000 people (29)
Jesus proclaims himself as the bread of life (29)

Timeline of The Story

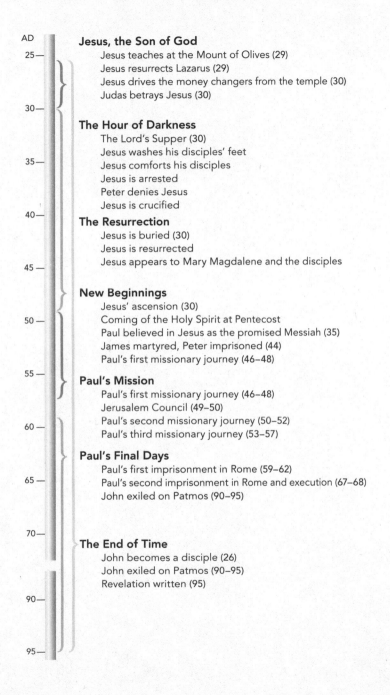

AD

25 —

30 —

35 —

40 —

45 —

50 —

55 —

60 —

65 —

70 —

90 —

95 —

Jesus, the Son of God
- Jesus teaches at the Mount of Olives (29)
- Jesus resurrects Lazarus (29)
- Jesus drives the money changers from the temple (30)
- Judas betrays Jesus (30)

The Hour of Darkness
- The Lord's Supper (30)
- Jesus washes his disciples' feet
- Jesus comforts his disciples
- Jesus is arrested
- Peter denies Jesus
- Jesus is crucified

The Resurrection
- Jesus is buried (30)
- Jesus is resurrected
- Jesus appears to Mary Magdalene and the disciples

New Beginnings
- Jesus' ascension (30)
- Coming of the Holy Spirit at Pentecost
- Paul believed in Jesus as the promised Messiah (35)
- James martyred, Peter imprisoned (44)
- Paul's first missionary journey (46–48)

Paul's Mission
- Paul's first missionary journey (46–48)
- Jerusalem Council (49–50)
- Paul's second missionary journey (50–52)
- Paul's third missionary journey (53–57)

Paul's Final Days
- Paul's first imprisonment in Rome (59–62)
- Paul's second imprisonment in Rome and execution (67–68)
- John exiled on Patmos (90–95)

The End of Time
- John becomes a disciple (26)
- John exiled on Patmos (90–95)
- Revelation written (95)

JESUS' BIRTH AND MINISTRY

MATTHEW–JOHN

WELCOME

None of us likes to wait. We get impatient at traffic lights. We get edgy when the line at the grocery store doesn't seem to move. We get irritated when people talk too slowly and won't get to the point. We don't like the inconvenience of having to wait for just a few minutes. But no amount of waiting on our part compares to what the people of Israel had endured. By the time the events of the New Testament unfold, they had been waiting *400 years* for the fulfillment of Isaiah's prophecy that a king would reign on David's throne and over his kingdom (Isaiah 9:7). Four hundred years is a long time to wait . . . and when their promised king did finally arrive, he was nothing like the figure from their Scriptures that they were expecting.

1

VIDEO TEACHING NOTES

Welcome to session one of *God the Savior*. If this is your first time together as a group, take a moment to introduce your-selves. Watch the video (see the streaming video access pro-vided on the inside front cover) and use the following outline to record some of the main points. The answer key is found at the end of the session.

- Jesus' life is filled with _____ from the begin-ning—illegitimate child, scandalous teaching, and a scandalous death on a Roman cross. Even his _____ would end up leading scandalous lives.

- The one in the womb of Mary has never been _____ by the seed of a man but by the Holy Spirit. This means the _____ _____ has not been transmitted to the child in her womb. He had been conceived without sin.

- *Immanuel* means "_____ _____ _____." The baby growing in Mary's womb is none other than God himself. He is leaving the upper story to not only be with us in the _____ _____ but to actually become one of us.

- The only place Mary and Joseph could find to de-liver God was a cave-like _____ behind one of the local Bethlehem inns. How unfortunate that the best we could do for the arrival of _____ into our world was a birth in a barn!

- But in the upper story, God wanted Jesus to be born in a manger. To fulfill _____, Jesus had to be born in Bethlehem in humble circumstances.

- We want all the people in our lives to see Jesus because his birth is not the _____ of a scandal but a _____ to our scandal—to our sin.

GETTING STARTED

Begin your discussion by reciting the following key verse and key idea together as a group. Now try to state the key verse from memory. On your first attempt, use your notes if you need help. On your second attempt, try to state it completely from memory.

Key Verse: "The Word became flesh and made his dwelling among us. We have seen his glory, the glory of the one and only Son, who came from the Father, full of grace and truth" (John 1:14).

Key Idea: Every story of Israel, including 353 Old Testament prophecies, have pointed to this day of Jesus' birth. It begins when the Lord orchestrates an empire-wide census that moves Mary and Joseph to Bethlehem in time for the delivery. Jesus is not born of man, but of God, and is the second man to walk on earth without sin in his nature. But unlike Adam, the first man, Jesus will *remain* sinless. His ministry is announced by John the Baptist, who proclaims that he is the Lamb of God who takes away the sin of the world. John thus makes the connection that the Passover lamb who saved the firstborn sons of Israel from the angel of death was really a symbol foreshadowing the coming of Jesus.

GROUP DISCUSSION

Take a few minutes with your group members to discuss what you just watched and explore these concepts in Scripture.

1. What part of this week's teaching encouraged or challenged you the most? Why?

_____

_____

_____

2. How was Jesus' life filled with scandal in the lower story?

_____

_____

_____

3. What do you believe is the significance of Jesus being born of the Holy Spirit?

_____

_____

_____

4. What do you learn about Joseph through his encounter with the angel?

_____

_____

_____

_____

_____

5. Why did God, in the upper story, want Jesus to be born in a stable in Bethlehem?

_____

_____

_____

_____

6. What is your biggest takeaway as you reflect on what you learned this week?

_____

_____

_____

_____

CLOSING PRAYER

One of the most important things we can do together in community is to pray for each other. This is not simply a closing prayer to end your group time but a portion of time to share prayer requests and life, to review how God has answered past prayers, and to actually pray for one another. Use the space below to record prayer requests and praises. Also, make sure to pray by name for people God might add to your group—especially your neighbors.

Name   Request/Praise

_____   _____

_____   _____

_____   _____

_____   _____

_____   _____

_____   _____

_____   _____

——— **FOR NEXT WEEK** ———

Next week, we will look at the story of the beginning of Jesus' surprisingly quiet entry into the public part of his earthly ministry. Before your next group meeting, be sure to read through the following personal study, complete the exercises, and memorize the key verse for the session.

VIDEO NOTES ANSWER KEY
scandal, disciples / conceived, sin nature / "God with us,"
lower story / stable, God / prophecy / result, solution

PERSONAL STUDY

Every session in this guide contains a personal study to help you make meaningful connections between your life and what you are learning each week. Take some time after your group meeting each week to read through this section and complete the personal study. In total, it should take about one hour to complete. Some people like to spread it out, devoting about ten to fifteen minutes a day. Others choose one larger block of time during the week to work through it in one sitting. There is no right or wrong way to do this! Just choose a plan that best fits your needs and schedule and then allow the Scripture to take root in your heart.

KNOW THE STORY

He walked with Adam and Eve in the garden. He spoke to Moses in the fire of a burning bush. He guided Israel in a cloud by day and fire by night. He sat enthroned over the ark of the covenant in the tabernacle and temple. But all of these were just the warm-up for the main act. Now, to fulfill the upper-story plan of providing a solution to humankind's sin, God would intervene directly into the lower story by becoming a human. Fully God . . . and yet fully man.

> *In the beginning was the Word, and the Word was with God, and the Word was God. He was with God in the beginning.*

Through him all things were made; without him nothing was made that has been made. In him was life, and that life was the light of all mankind. The light shines in the darkness, and the darkness has not overcome it.

There was a man sent from God whose name was John. He came as a witness to testify concerning that light, so that through him all might believe. He himself was not the light; he came only as a witness to the light.

The true light that gives light to everyone was coming into the world. He was in the world, and though the world was made through him, the world did not recognize him. He came to that which was his own, but his own did not receive him. Yet to all who did receive him, to those who believed in his name, he gave the right to become children of God—children born not of natural descent, nor of human decision or a husband's will, but born of God.

The Word became flesh and made his dwelling among us. We have seen his glory, the glory of the one and only Son, who came from the Father, full of grace and truth (John 1:1–14).

This is how the birth of Jesus the Messiah came about: His mother Mary was pledged to be married to Joseph, but before they came together, she was found to be pregnant through the Holy Spirit. Because Joseph her husband was faithful to the law, and yet did not want to expose her to public disgrace, he had in mind to divorce her quietly.

But after he had considered this, an angel of the Lord appeared to him in a dream and said, "Joseph son of David, do not be afraid to take Mary home as your wife, because what is conceived in her is from the Holy Spirit. She will give birth to a son, and you are to give him the name Jesus, because he will save his people from their sins."

All this took place to fulfill what the Lord had said through the prophet: "The virgin will conceive and give birth to a son, and they will call him Immanuel" (which means "God with us").

When Joseph woke up, he did what the angel of the Lord had commanded him and took Mary home as his wife. But he did not consummate their marriage until she gave birth to a son. And he gave him the name Jesus (Matthew 1:18–25).

In those days Caesar Augustus issued a decree that a census should be taken of the entire Roman world. (This was the first census that took place while Quirinius was governor of Syria.) And everyone went to their own town to register.

So Joseph also went up from the town of Nazareth in Galilee to Judea, to Bethlehem the town of David, because he belonged to the house and line of David. He went there to register with Mary, who was pledged to be married to him and was expecting a child. While they were there, the time came for the baby to be born, and she gave birth to her first-born, a son.

And there were shepherds living out in the fields nearby, keeping watch over their flocks at night. An angel of the Lord appeared to them, and the glory of the Lord shone around them, and they were terrified. But the angel said to them, "Do not be afraid. I bring you good news that will cause great joy for all the people. Today in the town of David a Savior has been born to you; he is the Messiah, the Lord. This will be a sign to you: You will find a baby wrapped in cloths and lying in a manger."

Suddenly a great company of the heavenly host appeared with the angel, praising God and saying, "Glory to God in the highest heaven, and on earth peace to those on whom his favor rests."

When the angels had left them and gone into heaven, the shepherds said to one another, "Let's go to Bethlehem and see this thing that has happened, which the Lord has told us about" (Luke 2:1–15).

The beginning of the good news about Jesus the Messiah, the Son of God, as it is written in Isaiah the prophet:

> *"I will send my messenger ahead of you,*
> *who will prepare your way"—*
> *"a voice of one calling in the wilderness,*
> *'Prepare the way for the Lord,*
> *make straight paths for him.'"*

And so John the Baptist appeared in the wilderness, preaching a baptism of repentance for the forgiveness of sins. The whole Judean countryside and all the people of Jerusalem went out to him. Confessing their sins, they were baptized by him in the Jordan River. John wore clothing made of camel's hair, with a leather belt around his waist, and he ate locusts and wild honey. And this was his message: "After me comes the one more powerful than I, the straps of whose sandals I am not worthy to stoop down and untie. I baptize you with water, but he will baptize you with the Holy Spirit."

At that time Jesus came from Nazareth in Galilee and was baptized by John in the Jordan. Just as Jesus was coming up out of the water, he saw heaven being torn open and the Spirit descending on him like a dove. And a voice came from heaven: "You are my Son, whom I love; with you I am well pleased" (Mark 1:1–11).

Jesus, full of the Holy Spirit, left the Jordan and was led by the Spirit into the wilderness, where for forty days he was tempted by the devil. He ate nothing during those days, and at the end of them he was hungry.

The devil said to him, "If you are the Son of God, tell this stone to become bread."

Jesus answered, "It is written: 'Man shall not live on bread alone.'"

The devil led him up to a high place and showed him in an instant all the kingdoms of the world. And he said to him, "I will give you all their authority and splendor; it has been given to me, and I can give it to anyone I want to. If you worship me, it will all be yours."

Jesus answered, "It is written: 'Worship the Lord your God and serve him only.'"

The devil led him to Jerusalem and had him stand on the highest point of the temple. "If you are the Son of God," he said, "throw yourself down from here. For it is written:

> *"'He will command his angels concerning you*
> *to guard you carefully;*
> *they will lift you up in their hands,*
> *so that you will not strike your foot against a stone.'"*

Jesus answered, "It is said: 'Do not put the Lord your God to the test.'"(Luke 4:1–12).

1. How does John, in his Gospel, describe the coming of Jesus into the world?

2. What was Joseph's initial plan when he learned of Mary's pregnancy?

3. What events led to Jesus being born in Bethlehem in fulfillment of prophecy?

4. What did John the Baptist proclaim about the coming Messiah?

5. What strategies did Satan employ to tempt Jesus in the wilderness?

_____

_____

_____

_____

_____

UNDERSTAND THE STORY

The doctrine of the incarnation, the eternal God entering the limitations of time and space and being born as a human being, lies at the heart of the Christian faith. In what can only be described as a mind-bending mystery, the child born in a manger and known to us as Jesus Christ is one person with two natures: fully human but also fully divine. While the many things that Jesus said revealed God in a way that no other words could, it was the Word himself who was the fullest revelation. As Paul wrote, "The Son is the image of the invisible God.... He is before all things, and in him all things hold together" (Colossians 1:15, 17).

Each of the four Gospels present a distinct understanding of Jesus. Matthew presents Jesus as a king, which underscores the fulfillment of God's promise to David to establish his descendant on an eternal throne. Mark presents Jesus as a servant, which emphasizes his humility as he goes about the business of his heavenly Father. Luke presents Jesus as a man, which highlights the Savior's common bond to all people. As Paul would later write, "He made himself nothing by taking the very nature of a servant, being made in human likeness. And being found in appearance as a man, he humbled himself" (Philippians 2:7–8).

John presents Jesus as a member of the Trinity—preexistent in eternity with all the power and authority of the Godhead. He takes great care to explain exactly who Jesus is: "the Word was God" (John 1:1). Our words come from us and express our identity. Identifying Jesus as "the Word" of God, who was God and was eternally with God, is equivalent to calling Jesus "God." God himself entered the story as a human being—and something new has happened, something we haven't seen since the beginning of time!

1. What do the stories you have read this week reveal about Jesus' identity?

_____

_____

_____

_____

2. How will these stories help you to better understand Jesus' nature?

_____

_____

_____

_____

LIVE THE STORY

Early in Jesus' ministry, while he was in Jerusalem, he received an unexpected visit from a Pharisee named Nicodemus. During their conversation, Jesus revealed God's plan for restoring us into a relationship with him. He told Nicodemus that in order to be a part of the divine community, he had to be "born again." Jesus then offered Nicodemus one of the clearest declarations of who he was and why he came down to this earth: "For God so loved the world that he gave his one and only Son, that whoever believes in him shall not perish but have eternal life" (John 3:16). We live "down here," in all the ordinary messiness of life, including what appears to be the final stop—*death*. But Jesus, who was "up there," came down to defeat death for us so that we can live eternally with him. All we have to do is believe.

1. How have you responded to Jesus' instruction to repent and be born again?

2. What is one action you will take this week to put what you've learned into practice?

TELL THE STORY

The goal of this study is not only for you to understand the story of the Bible but also for you to share it with others. So, one day this week around a meal or your dinner table, have an intentional conversation about the topic of this session with family or friends. During your time together, read Matthew 3:13–17, and then use the following question for discussion:

> *Why do you think it would be important for Jesus to hear his Father's blessing?*

Ask God this week to help you fully embrace the story of Jesus' birth and early ministry. Also, spend a few minutes each day committing the key verse to memory: "The Word became flesh and made his dwelling among us. We have seen his glory, the glory of the one and only Son, who came from the Father, full of grace and truth" (John 1:14).

JESUS, THE SON OF GOD

MATTHEW–JOHN

WELCOME

Have you ever met someone and known almost immediately that he or she was somebody special? I'm talking about a person you meet for the first time who has an extraordinary personality—a commanding presence that draws people to them. This is the effect Jesus had on people. He was more than just the son of a humble carpenter from Nazareth. One of the qualities that stood out and attracted attention was the way he taught about God. He told parables—stories that communicated truth in ways that the reading of the law could never match. He also performed miracles—calming a stormy sea, healing the sick, casting out demons, raising the dead to life. But Jesus said he was more than just a great teacher, physician, or miracle worker. As we will examine in this session, to the people's dismay, he claimed that he was also the Son of God.

——— VIDEO TEACHING NOTES ———

Welcome to session two of *God the Savior*. If there are any new members in your group, take a moment to introduce yourselves to each other. Spend a few minutes sharing any insights or questions about last week's personal study. Then watch the video (see the streaming video access provided on the inside front cover) and use the following outline to record some of the main points. The answer key is found at the end of the session.

- We read that Jesus was a master teacher, but his primary _____ was not a teacher. He was a miracle worker and healer, but his primary _____ wasn't a miracle worker or a physician. He was truly no ordinary man.

- Halfway through the festival in Jerusalem, Jesus got up and started to teach. The people asked, "How did this man get such _____ without having been taught?" Good question that demands an _____.

- Jesus not only told the people that he was around before _____ but also called himself "I Am"—the name for _____. They were ready to stone him.

- Jesus gets on a _____ and rides it into Jerusalem. What is he trying to say? What clue is he giving? He is fulfilling the prophecy of Zechariah in the Old Testament, who told us the _____ to come would do just this.

- Most people likely thought the Messiah would become their _____ and restore them to political greatness over Rome—a mere lower story accomplishment. But God had a greater _____ for Jesus—a higher, upper story assignment.

- Everything in the life and stories of Israel pointed to Jesus' coming. God's plan for him was to ____. He was going to pay for our sins so we can be made right with God and come back into a personal _____ with him.

GETTING STARTED

Begin your discussion by reciting the following key verses and key idea together as a group. Now try to state the key verses from memory. On your first attempt, use your notes if you need help. On your second attempt, try to state them completely from memory.

Key Verses: "I am the way and the truth and the life. No one comes to the Father except through me. If you really know me, you will know my Father as well. From now on, you do know him and have seen him" (John 14:6–7).

Key Idea: The ministry of Jesus is now in full motion. Jesus' teachings give people a glimpse of God's kingdom and vision for the life he intended them to have. Jesus' healing ministry not only shows mercy to the recipients but also authenticates his identity. He is no ordinary man but the Savior of the world. He is God! Yet the people do not understand what kind of king he has come to be—a suffering king—and what kind of kingdom he will rule—an eternal one.

GROUP DISCUSSION

Take a few minutes with your group members to discuss what you just watched and explore these concepts in Scripture.

1. What part of this week's teaching encouraged or challenged you the most? Why?

_____

_____

_____

_____

_____

2. How did the people of Jesus' day tend to view him?

_____

_____

_____

_____

_____

3. What are some of the clues that Jesus provided about his true identity?

_____

_____

_____

_____

4. What was the significance of Jesus entering Jerusalem riding on a donkey?

_____

_____

_____

_____

5. What did Jesus reveal was God's upper story plan for the Messiah to fulfill?

_____

_____

_____

_____

6. What is your biggest takeaway as you reflect on what you learned this week?

_____

_____

_____

_____

—— CLOSING PRAYER ——

End your group time by sharing prayer requests, reviewing how God has answered past prayers, and praying for one another. Use the space below to record any requests and praises. Also, make sure to pray for people God might add to your group—especially your neighbors.

Name   Request/Praise

_____   _____

_____   _____

_____   _____

_____   _____

_____   _____

—— FOR NEXT WEEK ——

Next week, we will look at the story of Jesus' death and how all of eternity was changed by this one act of sacrifice. Before your next group meeting, be sure to read through the following personal study, complete the exercises, and memorize the key verses for the session.

VIDEO NOTES ANSWER KEY

occupation, occupation / learning, answer / Abraham,
God / donkey, Messiah / king, plan / die, relationship

PERSONAL STUDY

Take some time after your group meeting this week to read through this section and complete the personal study. In total, it should take about one hour to complete. Allow the Scripture to take root in your heart as you review the story of Jesus' growing popularity in his ministry.

KNOW THE STORY

Jesus' ministry was composed of several different but complementary elements. He was always preaching, and his messages were always in some way about the kingdom of God. Jesus' ministry was also infused with miracles. These miracles served as signposts directing the attention of those watching to the day when all things would be made new. But Jesus was more than just a great teacher and a miracle worker. He was also the Messiah . . . the Son of the living God.

> *Jesus and his disciples went on to the villages around Caesarea Philippi. On the way he asked them, "Who do people say I am?"*
>
> *They replied, "Some say John the Baptist; others say Elijah; and still others, one of the prophets."*
>
> *"But what about you?" he asked. "Who do you say I am?"*
>
> *Peter answered, "You are the Messiah."*

Jesus warned them not to tell anyone about him.

He then began to teach them that the Son of Man must suffer many things and be rejected by the elders, the chief priests and the teachers of the law, and that he must be killed and after three days rise again. He spoke plainly about this, and Peter took him aside and began to rebuke him.

But when Jesus turned and looked at his disciples, he rebuked Peter. "Get behind me, Satan!" he said. "You do not have in mind the concerns of God, but merely human concerns."

Then he called the crowd to him along with his disciples and said: "Whoever wants to be my disciple must deny themselves and take up their cross and follow me. For whoever wants to save their life will lose it, but whoever loses their life for me and for the gospel will save it. What good is it for someone to gain the whole world, yet forfeit their soul? Or what can anyone give in exchange for their soul? If anyone is ashamed of me and my words in this adulterous and sinful generation, the Son of Man will be ashamed of them when he comes in his Father's glory with the holy angels" (Mark 8:27–38).

After this, Jesus went around in Galilee. He did not want to go about in Judea because the Jewish leaders there were looking for a way to kill him. But when the Jewish Festival of Tabernacles was near, Jesus' brothers said to him, "Leave Galilee and go to Judea, so that your disciples there may see the works you do. No one who wants to become a public figure acts in secret. Since you are doing these things, show yourself to the world." For even his own brothers did not believe in him.

Therefore Jesus told them, "My time is not yet here; for you any time will do. The world cannot hate you, but it hates me because I testify that its works are evil. You go to the festival. I am not going up to this festival, because my time has not yet fully come." After he had said this, he stayed in Galilee.

However, after his brothers had left for the festival, he went also, not publicly, but in secret. Now at the festival the Jewish leaders were watching for Jesus and asking, "Where is he?"

Among the crowds there was widespread whispering about him. Some said, "He is a good man."

Others replied, "No, he deceives the people." But no one would say anything publicly about him for fear of the leaders.

Not until halfway through the festival did Jesus go up to the temple courts and begin to teach. The Jews there were amazed and asked, "How did this man get such learning without having been taught?"

Jesus answered, "My teaching is not my own. It comes from the one who sent me. Anyone who chooses to do the will of God will find out whether my teaching comes from God or whether I speak on my own" (John 7:1–17).

When Jesus spoke again to the people, he said, "I am the light of the world. Whoever follows me will never walk in darkness, but will have the light of life."

The Pharisees challenged him, "Here you are, appearing as your own witness; your testimony is not valid."

Jesus answered, "Even if I testify on my own behalf, my testimony is valid, for I know where I came from and where I am going. But you have no idea where I come from or where

I am going. You judge by human standards; I pass judgment on no one. But if I do judge, my decisions are true, because I am not alone. I stand with the Father, who sent me. In your own Law it is written that the testimony of two witnesses is true. I am one who testifies for myself; my other witness is the Father, who sent me."

Then they asked him, "Where is your father?"

"You do not know me or my Father," Jesus replied. "If you knew me, you would know my Father also." He spoke these words while teaching in the temple courts near the place where the offerings were put. Yet no one seized him, because his hour had not yet come (John 8:12–20).

The Jews answered him, "Aren't we right in saying that you are a Samaritan and demon-possessed?"

"I am not possessed by a demon," said Jesus, "but I honor my Father and you dishonor me. I am not seeking glory for myself; but there is one who seeks it, and he is the judge. Very truly I tell you, whoever obeys my word will never see death."

At this they exclaimed, "Now we know that you are demon-possessed! Abraham died and so did the prophets, yet you say that whoever obeys your word will never taste death. Are you greater than our father Abraham? He died, and so did the prophets. Who do you think you are?"

Jesus replied, "If I glorify myself, my glory means nothing. My Father, whom you claim as your God, is the one who glorifies me. Though you do not know him, I know him. If I said I did not, I would be a liar like you, but I do know him and obey his word. Your father Abraham rejoiced at the thought of seeing my day; he saw it and was glad."

"You are not yet fifty years old," they said to him, "and you have seen Abraham!"

"Very truly I tell you," Jesus answered, "before Abraham was born, I am!" At this, they picked up stones to stone him, but Jesus hid himself, slipping away from the temple grounds (John 8:48–59).

As they approached Jerusalem and came to Bethphage and Bethany at the Mount of Olives, Jesus sent two of his disciples, saying to them, "Go to the village ahead of you, and just as you enter it, you will find a colt tied there, which no one has ever ridden. Untie it and bring it here. If anyone asks you, 'Why are you doing this?' say, 'The Lord needs it and will send it back here shortly.'"

They went and found a colt outside in the street, tied at a doorway. As they untied it, some people standing there asked, "What are you doing, untying that colt?" They answered as Jesus had told them to, and the people let them go. When they brought the colt to Jesus and threw their cloaks over it, he sat on it. Many people spread their cloaks on the road, while others spread branches they had cut in the fields. Those who went ahead and those who followed shouted,

> *"Hosanna!"*
> *"Blessed is he who comes in the name of the Lord!"*
> *"Blessed is the coming kingdom of our father David!"*
> *"Hosanna in the highest heaven!"*

Jesus entered Jerusalem and went into the temple courts. He looked around at everything, but since it was already late, he went out to Bethany with the Twelve (Mark 11:1–11).

1. What did Jesus explain to the disciples about what had to happen to the Messiah? Why do you think this caused Peter to take Jesus aside and rebuke him?

2. What reason did Jesus give for not wanting to go to the Festival of Tabernacles?

3. How did the religious leaders respond to Jesus' claim to be God?

4. What statement did Jesus make that caused the religious leaders to want to kill him?

5. How did the people respond to Jesus when he entered Jerusalem?

_____

_____

_____

_____

_____

UNDERSTAND THE STORY

Each of the Gospels gifts us with a biography of Jesus, sharing the things he did and said. However, the central point of each Gospel is not simply to convey information about what Jesus did and said but also to bring us to grips regarding Jesus' *identity*. The Gospels, especially the first three (called Synoptics), take time to drop hints along the way. Each is written to force us to scratch ours heads and ask, "Who is this man?" They do this by allowing us to see Jesus through several perspectives. Sometimes we are with the disciples, wondering what Jesus could possibly mean. Sometimes we are with a needy person, coming to Jesus for help. Sometimes we are meant to see ourselves in the less favorable characters.

As Jesus moves closer to the cross, the question of his identity takes on more urgency. The disciples are beginning to make statements about him. The crowds are wondering. The religious leaders are furious that Jesus himself is making statements such as, "Before Abraham was born, I am!" (John 8:58). For them, it sounded suspiciously like Jesus was calling himself the "I AM" who spoke from the burning bush in Sinai.

It is becoming clearer and clearer that Jesus will not allow people simply to call him a good teacher.

Peter's confession, "You are the Messiah," represents the high-water mark in the history of human understanding up to that point. In those four words, Peter articulates the hope of the ages—even though his concept of how this would play out wasn't yet on target. For the first time in human history, God's prophesied Anointed One was clearly recognized. Peter's confession is complemented and undergirded when Jesus is transfigured, appears in all his glorious splendor, and the Father again speaks his pleasure over the Son.

1. What do the stories that you have read this week reveal about the importance of acknowledging Jesus as the Son of God?

2. How will these stories help you better understand the place Jesus deserves in your life?

LIVE THE STORY

We all must answer the question the disciples asked about Jesus: "What kind of man is this?" (Matthew 8:27). In the lower story, Jesus is a remarkable man whose teachings continue to provide a foundation for moral and ethical behavior. He was a good man who had a special place in his heart for the poor and oppressed. But his claim to be the Son of God requires us to make a choice. In the words of C.S. Lewis, we have to decide whether he is a "liar, lunatic, or Lord." Our eternal life depends on our declaration that Jesus *is* the Son of God and *is* the one who "takes away the sin of the world" (see John 1:29). It has always been God's upper Story message that he wants us to be "all in" with our faith in his Son.

1. How do you show that you have truly made Jesus the Lord of your life?

2. What is one action you will take this week to put what you've learned into practice?

───── TELL THE STORY ─────

One day this week around a meal or your dinner table, have a conversation about the topic of this session with family or friends. During your time together, read John 10:22–33, and then use the following question for discussion:

What are ways that we can listen to Jesus' voice in our lives?

Ask God this week to help you fully embrace the story of Jesus' impact in his ministry and the claims he made that he is the Son of God. Also, spend a few minutes each day committing the key verses to memory: "I am the way and the truth and the life. No one comes to the Father except through me. If you really know me, you will know my Father as well. From now on, you do know him and have seen him" (John 14:6–7).

THE HOUR OF DARKNESS

MATTHEW–JOHN

WELCOME

In every endeavor, there is the potential for the thrill of victory . . . or the agony of defeat. The disciples must have been feeling victorious and vindicated after they witnessed Jesus ride into Jerusalem on the back of a donkey in fulfillment of Isaiah's prophecy. The common people of the city had greeted him as if he were a king. They had scattered palm branches in front of him, which in Jewish culture was a symbol of victory. Finally, they would have their promised Messiah who would restore Israel to greatness—and maybe even lead them to overthrow Rome! What the disciples couldn't have known in the lower story is that God had something even greater in mind in the upper story. But to get there, they would first have to endure what seemed like the greatest agony of defeat when Jesus was put to death on a Roman cross.

VIDEO TEACHING NOTES

Welcome to session three of *God the Savior*. Spend a few minutes sharing any insights or questions about last week's personal study. Then watch the video (see the streaming video access provided on the inside front cover). The answer key is found at the end of the session.

- Chapter by chapter, God's plan of redemption has been unfolding. Every story in the life of _____ points to the first coming of Jesus. But what is Jesus, the Son of God, going to do to provide this _____ back to God?

- Jesus is taken before Caiaphas, the high priest. They are looking for _____ to convict him and kill him. Jesus gives them what they need, and they spit in his face, strike him on the face with their fists, and slap him.

- Jesus is placed on the cross and there dies. Those who crucify him in the lower story think, "He is _____." But this is not how it came down in the upper story. Jesus is being sacrificed as the Passover _____ of God.

- Jesus knew he would endure _____ and humiliation on the cross. The bigger deal is that all the sins of mankind would be transferred to him. Yet Jesus _____ his life to the upper story and went through with God's plan.

- Jesus' cry, "It is finished," isn't a declaration of defeat but of _____. Jesus is saying the work that he came to do has been completed. Sin has been _____ _____ once and for all for all people.

- We now have direct _____ to God through the shed blood of Christ. The curse of Adam has been lifted for all who believe in Jesus as the Son of God, the Messiah. Finally, the _____ back to God has come.

GETTING STARTED

Begin your discussion by reciting the following key verses and key idea together as a group. Now try to state the key verses from memory. On your first attempt, use your notes if you need help. On your second attempt, try to state them completely from memory.

Key Verses: "The curtain of the temple was torn in two. Jesus called out with a loud voice, 'Father, into your hands I commit my spirit.' When he had said this, he breathed his last" (Luke 23:45–46).

Key Idea: All hope in Jesus being the promised Messiah now seems to be lost. One of his disciples rats him out for thirty pieces of silver. His most trusted disciple betrays him in his hour of need. The rest scatter and hide. The Jewish leaders demand that he be crucified. The Romans consent and nail Jesus to a cross. In the lower story, it looks like Jesus is finished. But in the upper story, he has actually finished what God sent him to accomplish. The plan set in motion back in the Garden of Eden is complete, and salvation is available to all nations. Jesus, the Son of God, has died for the sins of the world, once and for all.

GROUP DISCUSSION

Take a few minutes with your group members to discuss what you just watched and explore these concepts in Scripture.

1. What part of this week's teaching encouraged or challenged you the most? Why?

2. What are some of the events in the lower story that led to Jesus' crucifixion?

3. What is significant about the season of year in which Jesus' crucifixion took place?

_____

_____

_____

_____

4. What was Jesus declaring on the cross when he said that "it is finished"?

_____

_____

_____

_____

5. What was God declaring upon Jesus' death when he tore the curtain in the temple?

_____

_____

_____

_____

6. What is your biggest takeaway as you reflect on what you learned this week?

_____

_____

_____

_____

CLOSING PRAYER

End your group time by sharing prayer requests, reviewing how God has answered past prayers, and praying for one another. Use the space below to record any requests and praises. Also, make sure to pray for people God might add to your group—especially your neighbors.

Name   Request/Praise

_____   _____
_____   _____
_____   _____
_____   _____
_____   _____

FOR NEXT WEEK

Next week, we will look at the story of the amazing resurrection of Jesus and how he had power over death. Before your next group meeting, be sure to read through the following personal study, complete the exercises, and memorize the key verses for the session.

VIDEO NOTES ANSWER KEY

Israel, way / evidence / finished, Lamb / pain,
aligned / victory, paid for / access, way

PERSONAL STUDY

Take some time after your group meeting this week to read through this section and complete the personal study. In total, it should take about one hour to complete. Allow the Scripture to take root in your heart as you look at the story of Jesus' crucifixion on the cross.

KNOW THE STORY

As we have seen, God never wanted to be separated from his people. So he put a plan in place to get his people back. It appeared to the Jewish people who lined the streets of Jerusalem that this plan had culminated in a triumphal entry by Jesus. But what would he do next? Fight Rome? Set up a power base? No, he would die on a cross. This begins with the betrayal of Judas, one of his own disciples, and a trial by "kangaroo court" before Caiaphas, the high priest. And Jesus allows them to frame him. It is part of the plan. It *has* to happen this way.

> *Then one of the Twelve—the one called Judas Iscariot—went to the chief priests and asked, "What are you willing to give me if I deliver him over to you?" So they counted out for him thirty pieces of silver. From then on Judas watched for an opportunity to hand him over.*

On the first day of the Festival of Unleavened Bread, the disciples came to Jesus and asked, "Where do you want us to make preparations for you to eat the Passover?"

He replied, "Go into the city to a certain man and tell him, 'The Teacher says: My appointed time is near. I am going to celebrate the Passover with my disciples at your house.' " So the disciples did as Jesus had directed them and prepared the Passover.

When evening came, Jesus was reclining at the table with the Twelve. And while they were eating, he said, "Truly I tell you, one of you will betray me."

They were very sad and began to say to him one after the other, "Surely you don't mean me, Lord?"

Jesus replied, "The one who has dipped his hand into the bowl with me will betray me. The Son of Man will go just as it is written about him. But woe to that man who betrays the Son of Man! It would be better for him if he had not been born."

Then Judas, the one who would betray him, said, "Surely you don't mean me, Rabbi?"

Jesus answered, "You have said so" (Matthew 26:14–25).

Then Jesus went with his disciples to a place called Gethsemane, and he said to them, "Sit here while I go over there and pray." He took Peter and the two sons of Zebedee along with him, and he began to be sorrowful and troubled. Then he said to them, "My soul is overwhelmed with sorrow to the point of death. Stay here and keep watch with me."

Going a little farther, he fell with his face to the ground and prayed, "My Father, if it is possible, may this cup be taken from me. Yet not as I will, but as you will" (Matthew 26:36–39).

Then Pilate took Jesus and had him flogged. The soldiers twisted together a crown of thorns and put it on his head. They clothed him in a purple robe and went up to him again and again, saying, "Hail, king of the Jews!" And they slapped him in the face.

Once more Pilate came out and said to the Jews gathered there, "Look, I am bringing him out to you to let you know that I find no basis for a charge against him." When Jesus came out wearing the crown of thorns and the purple robe, Pilate said to them, "Here is the man!"

As soon as the chief priests and their officials saw him, they shouted, "Crucify! Crucify!"

But Pilate answered, "You take him and crucify him. As for me, I find no basis for a charge against him."

The Jewish leaders insisted, "We have a law, and according to that law he must die, because he claimed to be the Son of God."

When Pilate heard this, he was even more afraid, and he went back inside the palace. "Where do you come from?" he asked Jesus, but Jesus gave him no answer. "Do you refuse to speak to me?" Pilate said. "Don't you realize I have power either to free you or to crucify you?"

Jesus answered, "You would have no power over me if it were not given to you from above. Therefore the one who handed me over to you is guilty of a greater sin."

From then on, Pilate tried to set Jesus free, but the Jewish leaders kept shouting, "If you let this man go, you are no friend of Caesar. Anyone who claims to be a king opposes Caesar."

When Pilate heard this, he brought Jesus out and sat down on the judge's seat at a place known as the Stone Pavement (which in Aramaic is Gabbatha). It was the day of Preparation of the Passover; it was about noon.

"Here is your king," Pilate said to the Jews.

But they shouted, "Take him away! Take him away! Crucify him!"

"Shall I crucify your king?" Pilate asked.

"We have no king but Caesar," the chief priests answered.

Finally Pilate handed him over to them to be crucified (John 19:1–16).

Later, knowing that everything had now been finished, and so that Scripture would be fulfilled, Jesus said, "I am thirsty." A jar of wine vinegar was there, so they soaked a sponge in it, put the sponge on a stalk of the hyssop plant, and lifted it to Jesus' lips. When he had received the drink, Jesus said, "It is finished." With that, he bowed his head and gave up his spirit.

Now it was the day of Preparation, and the next day was to be a special Sabbath. Because the Jewish leaders did not want the bodies left on the crosses during the Sabbath, they asked Pilate to have the legs broken and the bodies taken down. The soldiers therefore came and broke the legs of the first man who had been crucified with Jesus, and then those of the other. But when they came to Jesus and found that he was already dead, they did not break his legs. Instead, one of the soldiers pierced Jesus' side with a spear, bringing a sudden flow of blood and water. The man who saw it has given testimony, and his testimony is true. He knows that he tells the truth, and he testifies so that you also may believe. These things happened so that the scripture would be fulfilled: "Not one of his bones will be broken," and, as another scripture says, "They will look on the one they have pierced" (John 19:28–37).

From noon until three in the afternoon darkness came over all the land. About three in the afternoon Jesus cried out in a loud voice, "Eli, Eli, lema sabachthani?" (which means "My God, my God, why have you forsaken me?").

When some of those standing there heard this, they said, "He's calling Elijah."

Immediately one of them ran and got a sponge. He filled it with wine vinegar, put it on a staff, and offered it to Jesus to drink. The rest said, "Now leave him alone. Let's see if Elijah comes to save him."

And when Jesus had cried out again in a loud voice, he gave up his spirit.

At that moment the curtain of the temple was torn in two from top to bottom. The earth shook, the rocks split and the tombs broke open. The bodies of many holy people who had died were raised to life. They came out of the tombs after Jesus' resurrection and went into the holy city and appeared to many people.

When the centurion and those with him who were guarding Jesus saw the earthquake and all that had happened, they were terrified, and exclaimed, "Surely he was the Son of God!"

Many women were there, watching from a distance. They had followed Jesus from Galilee to care for his needs. (Matthew 27:45–55).

1. What part did Judas play in God's upper story plan?

2. What decision did Jesus have to make in the Garden of Gethsemane?

3. Why was Pilate reluctant to sentence Jesus to death?

4. What is the significance in none of Jesus' bones being broken on the cross?

5. What caused those standing near the cross to acknowledge Jesus as the Son of God?

_____

_____

_____

_____

_____

UNDERSTAND THE STORY

Jesus was always clear about his mission: "I have come here to die, to give my life as a ransom for many" (see Mark 10:45). We must not forget this important truth about the death of Jesus: _he willingly walked to the cross._ The Jewish leaders may have worked the system and forced Pilate's hand, but the entire process was guided by the hand of God. From eternity this had been the plan. God's spotless Lamb was to be slain for the sins of the world.

In recent decades it has become fashionable to portray Jesus as a victim of social injustice. Some have said that Jesus was crushed under the thumb of the Romans. Others have seen Jesus' suffering as a divine identification with victims everywhere. But that is not what the Story reveals about Jesus' suffering. Jesus drank the cup of _God's_ judgment, not Pilate's. In fact, Jesus _became_ sin—identifying himself with our disobedience and rebellion—so that we might become the righteousness of God. As Paul later wrote, "God made him who had no sin to be sin for us, so that in him we might become the righteousness of God" (2 Corinthians 5:21).

In the lower story, Jesus' crucifixion was a disaster and a colossal failure. But in the upper story, it ushered in the victory that God had planned from the beginning of time. Christ willingly put himself in our place and chose to suffer the penalty of our sin for us. This truth disarms every pretense of the religious perfectionist and undercuts any other formula for our salvation. For as we look at the horror of the cross, we realize something: the only reason God would do things this way is if there were no other way to save us.

1. What do the stories you have read this week reveal about God's plan of salvation?

_____

_____

_____

_____

_____

_____

2. How will these stories help you better understand the gravity of sin and God's mercy?

_____

_____

_____

_____

_____

_____

—— LIVE THE STORY ——

God's upper story has been centered on providing the way for us to come back into a relationship with him. We could not make this happen in and of ourselves because of our sin nature, so God sent his Son to do for us what we could not do for ourselves. The sinless Son of God, the second person of the Trinity, took on flesh and died on the cross. So, what is our part in all of this in the lower story? Our part is to align ourselves with God's upper story and find our way back into the "garden." The only thing God asks of us is that we open our hands and accept his gift of forgiveness—to go all in with him. This simple act of faith of accepting Jesus' sacrifice for our sins reserves a place for us in his eternal home.

1. How do you respond when you consider this incredible offer of eternal life with God?

2. What is one action you will take this week to put what you've learned into practice?

TELL THE STORY

One day this week around a meal or your dinner table, have a conversation about the topic of this session with family or friends. During your time together, read Luke 22:54–62, and then use the following question for discussion:

How should we handle it when a close friend turns against us in some way?

Ask God this week to help you fully embrace the story of Jesus willingly giving his life for our sins. Also, spend a few minutes each day committing the key verses to memory: "The curtain of the temple was torn in two. Jesus called out with a loud voice, 'Father, into your hands I commit my spirit.' When he had said this, he breathed his last" (Luke 23:45–46).

THE RESURRECTION

MATTHEW–JOHN

WELCOME

The followers of Christ were running low on hope after experiencing the saddest day of their lives. Jesus, the man who had identified himself as God's own Son, had just been crucified alongside two common criminals. The authorities had declared him to be dead, his body had been taken down from the cross, and he had been placed in a tomb. On numerous occasions, Jesus had predicted his own death but had told his followers that he would rise again after three days. But in their lower story lives, his death seemed so final. All their hopes and dreams of Jesus being the Messiah had been dashed. So it was that when two women—both named Mary— went to the tomb to pay their respects, they were not expecting to find anything there but a deceased body. But instead what they encountered changed everything . . . *forever*.

VIDEO TEACHING NOTES

Welcome to session four of *God the Savior*. Spend a few minutes sharing any insights or questions about last week's personal study. Then watch the video (see the streaming video access provided on the inside front cover). The answer key is found at the end of the session.

- After Jesus' death, the disciples were _____ in the lower story. They had just lost their leader, their teacher. They were _____ the loss of the person who believed in them and gave them a life worth living on earth.

- Even though the disciples weren't expecting Jesus to _____ from the dead, there was a group who heard the rumor of Jesus' potential resurrection and took it seriously—the _____ who had Jesus crucified.

- When the women saw the _____ had been rolled away from the tomb, their first thought was not, "He has risen from the dead," but, "Where have they taken his body?" They are _____ who are missing their shepherd.

- Jesus painted the big picture for the disciples on the road to Emmaus. He started with _____ and went all the way through the _____, showing how everything pointed to his coming, his death, and his resurrection.

- All of those individual lower stories in the _____ _____ were contributing to the one upper story of God and his plan to get us back.

- We will no longer stand before the gravesides of people we have loved and _____ with no hope. If they have embraced this free gift of forgiveness, we will see each other again in the _____ of God to come.

GETTING STARTED

Begin your discussion by reciting the following key verses and key idea together as a group. Now try to state the key verses from memory. On your first attempt, use your notes if you need help. On your second attempt, try to state them completely from memory.

Key Verses: "Therefore go and make disciples of all nations, baptizing them in the name of the Father and of the Son and of the Holy Spirit, and teaching them to obey everything I have commanded you. And surely I am with you always, to the very end of the age" (Matthew 28:19–20).

Key Idea: Jesus came into our lower story world to represent us by taking on a perishable body. During his thirty-three years on earth, he resisted every temptation and, unlike Adam in the Garden of Eden, came out sinless. "The wages of sin is death" (Romans

6:23), but because Jesus wasn't a sinner, death could not keep him in the grave. His perishable body died, but three days later he rose from the dead to conquer death once and for all. God had kept his promise, and the way back to him was now open for all people from all nations.

GROUP DISCUSSION

Take a few minutes with your group members to discuss what you just watched and explore these concepts in Scripture.

1. What part of this week's teaching encouraged or challenged you the most? Why?

_____

_____

_____

_____

_____

2. Why did the Jewish religious leaders request a guard to be posted at Jesus' tomb?

_____

_____

_____

_____

_____

_____

3. For what reason did Mary Magdalene and Mary the mother of James go to Jesus' tomb?

_____

_____

_____

_____

4. What did Jesus reveal to the two disciples on the road to Emmaus?

_____

_____

_____

_____

5. What did Jesus say would be his disciples' next mission?

_____

_____

_____

_____

6. What is your biggest takeaway as you reflect on what you learned this week?

_____

_____

_____

_____

——— CLOSING PRAYER ———

End your group time by sharing prayer requests, reviewing how God has answered past prayers, and praying for one another. Use the space below to record any requests and praises. Also, make sure to pray for people God might add to your group—especially your neighbors.

Name   Request/Praise

_____   _____

_____   _____

_____   _____

_____   _____

_____   _____

——— FOR NEXT WEEK ———

New week, we will look at the story of the beginning of the church and how rapidly God expanded it during its early days. Before your next group meeting, be sure to read through the following personal study, complete the exercises, and memorize the key verses for the session.

VIDEO NOTES ANSWER KEY

wallowing, grieving / rise, religious leaders / stone, sheep / Moses, prophets/ Old Testament / grieve, garden

PERSONAL STUDY

Take some time after your group meeting this week to read through this section and complete the personal study. In total, it should take about one hour to complete. Allow the Scripture to take root in your heart as you review the story of Jesus conquering death and the grave.

KNOW THE STORY

The followers of Jesus were grieving the loss of the man they thought was the Messiah. One of those followers, Joseph of Arimathea, received permission to retrieve the body, prepare it for burial, and place it in a tomb. In one of those rest-of-the-story moments, a man named Nicodemus—the religious leader who had asked Jesus what it meant to be born again—brought seventy-five pounds of myrrh and aloe to apply to Jesus' body. It seems Nicodemus had gotten the message. But if he still had any lingering doubts, they would soon be erased . . . in three days.

> *Later, Joseph of Arimathea asked Pilate for the body of Jesus. Now Joseph was a disciple of Jesus, but secretly because he feared the Jewish leaders. With Pilate's permission, he came and took the body away. He was accompanied by Nicodemus, the man who earlier had visited Jesus at night. Nicodemus brought a mixture of myrrh and aloes, about seventy-five*

pounds. Taking Jesus' body, the two of them wrapped it, with the spices, in strips of linen. This was in accordance with Jewish burial customs. At the place where Jesus was crucified, there was a garden, and in the garden a new tomb, in which no one had ever been laid. Because it was the Jewish day of Preparation and since the tomb was nearby, they laid Jesus there (John 19:38–42).

As evening approached, there came a rich man from Arimathea, named Joseph, who had himself become a disciple of Jesus. Going to Pilate, he asked for Jesus' body, and Pilate ordered that it be given to him. Joseph took the body, wrapped it in a clean linen cloth, and placed it in his own new tomb that he had cut out of the rock. He rolled a big stone in front of the entrance to the tomb and went away. Mary Magdalene and the other Mary were sitting there opposite the tomb

The next day, the one after Preparation Day, the chief priests and the Pharisees went to Pilate. "Sir," they said, "we remember that while he was still alive that deceiver said, 'After three days I will rise again.' So give the order for the tomb to be made secure until the third day. Otherwise, his disciples may come and steal the body and tell the people that he has been raised from the dead. This last deception will be worse than the first."

"Take a guard," Pilate answered. "Go, make the tomb as secure as you know how." So they went and made the tomb secure by putting a seal on the stone and posting the guard (Matthew 27:57–66).

After the Sabbath, at dawn on the first day of the week, Mary Magdalene and the other Mary went to look at the tomb.

There was a violent earthquake, for an angel of the Lord came down from heaven and, going to the tomb, rolled back the stone and sat on it. His appearance was like lightning, and his clothes were white as snow. The guards were so afraid of him that they shook and became like dead men.

The angel said to the women, "Do not be afraid, for I know that you are looking for Jesus, who was crucified. He is not here; he has risen, just as he said. Come and see the place where he lay. Then go quickly and tell his disciples: 'He has risen from the dead and is going ahead of you into Galilee. There you will see him.' Now I have told you."

So the women hurried away from the tomb, afraid yet filled with joy, and ran to tell his disciples. Suddenly Jesus met them. "Greetings," he said. They came to him, clasped his feet and worshiped him. Then Jesus said to them, "Do not be afraid. Go and tell my brothers to go to Galilee; there they will see me."

While the women were on their way, some of the guards went into the city and reported to the chief priests everything that had happened. When the chief priests had met with the elders and devised a plan, they gave the soldiers a large sum of money, telling them, "You are to say, 'His disciples came during the night and stole him away while we were asleep.' If this report gets to the governor, we will satisfy him and keep you out of trouble." So the soldiers took the money and did as they were instructed. And this story has been widely circulated among the Jews to this very day (Matthew 28:1–15).

Early on the first day of the week, while it was still dark, Mary Magdalene went to the tomb and saw that the stone had been removed from the entrance. So she came running to Simon Peter and the other disciple, the one Jesus loved, and said,

"They have taken the Lord out of the tomb, and we don't know where they have put him!"

So Peter and the other disciple started for the tomb. Both were running, but the other disciple outran Peter and reached the tomb first. He bent over and looked in at the strips of linen lying there but did not go in. Then Simon Peter came along behind him and went straight into the tomb. He saw the strips of linen lying there, as well as the cloth that had been wrapped around Jesus' head. The cloth was still lying in its place, separate from the linen. Finally the other disciple, who had reached the tomb first, also went inside. He saw and believed. (They still did not understand from Scripture that Jesus had to rise from the dead.) Then the disciples went back to where they were staying.

Now Mary stood outside the tomb crying. As she wept, she bent over to look into the tomb and saw two angels in white, seated where Jesus' body had been, one at the head and the other at the foot.

They asked her, "Woman, why are you crying?"

"They have taken my Lord away," she said, "and I don't know where they have put him." At this, she turned around and saw Jesus standing there, but she did not realize that it was Jesus.

He asked her, "Woman, why are you crying? Who is it you are looking for?"

Thinking he was the gardener, she said, "Sir, if you have carried him away, tell me where you have put him, and I will get him."

Jesus said to her, "Mary."

She turned toward him and cried out in Aramaic, "Rabboni!" (which means "Teacher").

Jesus said, "Do not hold on to me, for I have not yet ascended to the Father. Go instead to my brothers and tell them, 'I am ascending to my Father and your Father, to my God and your God.'"

Mary Magdalene went to the disciples with the news: "I have seen the Lord!" And she told them that he had said these things to her (John 20:1–18).

Now that same day two of them were going to a village called Emmaus, about seven miles from Jerusalem. They were talking with each other about everything that had happened. As they talked and discussed these things with each other, Jesus himself came up and walked along with them; but they were kept from recognizing him.

He asked them, "What are you discussing together as you walk along?"

They stood still, their faces downcast. One of them, named Cleopas, asked him, "Are you the only one visiting Jerusalem who does not know the things that have happened there in these days?"

"What things?" he asked.

"About Jesus of Nazareth," they replied. "He was a prophet, powerful in word and deed before God and all the people. The chief priests and our rulers handed him over to be sentenced to death, and they crucified him; but we had hoped that he was the one who was going to redeem Israel. And what is more, it is the third day since all this took place. In addition, some of our women amazed us. They went to the tomb early this morning but didn't find his body. They came and told us that they had seen a vision of angels, who said he was alive. Then some of our companions went to the

tomb and found it just as the women had said, but they did not see Jesus."

He said to them, "How foolish you are, and how slow to believe all that the prophets have spoken! Did not the Messiah have to suffer these things and then enter his glory?" And beginning with Moses and all the Prophets, he explained to them what was said in all the Scriptures concerning himself.

As they approached the village to which they were going, Jesus continued on as if he were going farther. But they urged him strongly, "Stay with us, for it is nearly evening; the day is almost over." So he went in to stay with them.

When he was at the table with them, he took bread, gave thanks, broke it and began to give it to them. Then their eyes were opened and they recognized him, and he disappeared from their sight. They asked each other, "Were not our hearts burning within us while he talked with us on the road and opened the Scriptures to us?"

They got up and returned at once to Jerusalem. There they found the Eleven and those with them, assembled together and saying, "It is true! The Lord has risen and has appeared to Simon" (Luke 24:13–34).

Then the eleven disciples went to Galilee, to the mountain where Jesus had told them to go. When they saw him, they worshiped him; but some doubted. Then Jesus came to them and said, "All authority in heaven and on earth has been given to me. Therefore go and make disciples of all nations, baptizing them in the name of the Father and of the Son and of the Holy Spirit, and teaching them to obey everything I have commanded you. And surely I am with you always, to the very end of the age" (Matthew 28:16–20).

1. What events led to Jesus being placed in a tomb under a Roman guard?

2. What did the angel say to the two women when they approached the tomb?

3. What did Peter and John do when they heard that Jesus' tomb was empty?

4. How did the disciples on the road to Emmaus describe the recent events to Jesus?

5. What did Jesus proclaim about his authority after the resurrection?

_____

_____

_____

_____

UNDERSTAND THE STORY

The Gospel writers were careful to stress that Jesus was *really* dead. The Roman soldiers, skilled at determining the time of death by sight, confirmed this by piercing Jesus' side with a spear, penetrating his heart. John emphasizes in his Gospel account that "he tells the truth" about Jesus' death. He also repeatedly uses the word *body* to remind his readers that Jesus was physically dead: Joseph asked "for the body," they took "the body," they wrapped "the body" with spices, and the Pharisees feared the disciples might steal "the body."

But just as the Gospel writers are careful to state that Jesus really died, so they are also careful to offer strong support to prove that Jesus *really* rose from the dead. First, the tomb was empty. The moment the early Christians claimed that Jesus had risen, the religious leaders could have silenced them by simply pointing to the body lying in the tomb. But they could not. Second, the body was missing. The Gospel writers carefully describe details about the grave to emphasize something unusual had happened—the body had not just been stolen. Third, Jesus appeared to many people. More than 500 people repeatedly encountered the risen Christ.

But perhaps the most convincing proof of Jesus' resurrection is the dramatic change in his followers themselves. When Jesus was arrested, his disciples ran for their lives. They abandoned their teacher and fled into safety. Clearly, there were no heroes in this group of followers. So why in the world would these same disciples stand up—just a few months later—and risk their lives by publicly proclaiming a message they knew was a lie? Only fifty days following the resurrection, the same Peter who had been unwilling even to admit a passing acquaintance with Jesus would stand up in public and preach boldly in Jesus' name.

1. What do the stories you have read this week reveal about the importance of Jesus' resurrection in God's plan to redeem the world?

_____

_____

_____

_____

_____

2. How will these stories help you to better understand God's plans for your life?

_____

_____

_____

_____

_____

LIVE THE STORY

From a lower story perspective, death seems so final. But from an upper-story perspective, death is only the beginning. Jesus' perishable body died when he was crucified on the cross. But three days later, he rose from the grave with a new and imperishable body. He conquered death once and for all. Jesus' resurrection has provided us with the means to eternal life—and we, too, will one day be raised from the dead with a new imperishable body. As Paul explains, "The body that is sown is perishable, it is raised imperishable; it is sown in dishonor, it is raised in glory; it is sown in weakness, it is raised in power; it is sown a natural body, it is raised a spiritual body" (1 Corinthians 15:42–44). This is our hope and our destiny in Christ. Those who are transformed by faith in Jesus' death and resurrection have eternal life in Jesus. All of our failures and past sins are put to death and we become a brand-new creation in Christ.

1. How does this promise of eternal life motivate you to participate in God's plans for you to "go into all the world" and proclaim the message of salvation?

_____

_____

_____

_____

_____

_____

_____

2. What is one action you will take this week to put what you've learned into practice?

_____

_____

_____

_____

_____

_____

_____

_____

TELL THE STORY

One day this week around a meal or your dinner table, have a conversation about the topic of this session with family or friends. During your time together, read Mark 16:1–8, and then use the following question for discussion:

Why it is important for us to believe that Jesus actually rose from the dead?

Ask God this week to help you fully embrace the story of Jesus' miraculous resurrection. Also, spend a few minutes each day committing the key verses to memory: "Therefore go and make disciples of all nations, baptizing them in the name of the Father and of the Son and of the Holy Spirit, and teaching them to obey everything I have commanded you. And surely I am with you always, to the very end of the age" (Matthew 28:19–20).

Session 5

NEW BEGINNINGS

ACTS 1–12

WELCOME

Jesus began his ministry by forming a community of twelve disciples to travel with him and learn from him as he proclaimed the gospel or "good news" of God's salvation. Now, as Jesus' time on earth was drawing to a close, it was time for him to turn over the reins of that mission to those followers who had done life with him. They would be "witnesses" of this wonderful news and take bold risks to proclaim it to a hurting world. But in order to do this, Jesus knew they would need a supernatural power source. As we will discover in this session, this power would come in the form of the third person of the Godhead—the Holy Spirit—who would enter their lower story and give them the courage and guidance they needed to fulfill their calling.

VIDEO TEACHING NOTES

Welcome to session five of *God the Savior*. Spend a few minutes sharing any insights or questions about last week's personal study. Then watch the video (see the streaming video access provided on the inside front cover). The answer key is found at the end of the session.

- Jesus said that if we _____ our sin and accept his gift as full payment for it, we can become children of God. This is the gospel or "_____ _____."

- The disciples wanted to know if it was time for the _____ of God to be restored. Jesus told them not to worry about the timing of its arrival but to instead be focused on their new _____.

- The disciples are to be _____ to the fact that Jesus is alive. They are not so much called to *do* witnessing as they are called to ____ witnesses.

- The _____ _____ comes down like a fire and enters into the life of the disciples. They are charged with a newfound courage and _____. They open the doors they have been quarantined in and enter into the world of Jerusalem.

- The first church service was done completely over the evening _____ of the day. It was there they not only had a great feast but also they ate bread and drank of the cup, _____ the death of Christ and all that he did to change the outcome of their lives. They were a family.

- Those of us who have accepted the free gift of _____ in Christ have not only been forgiven but have also received the Holy Spirit to empower us to live this new life. We have become a part of this _____ _____ .

GETTING STARTED

Begin your discussion by reciting the following key verse and key idea together as a group. Now try to state the key verse from memory. On your first attempt, use your notes if you need help. On your second attempt, try to state it completely from memory.

Key Verse: "But you will receive power when the Holy Spirit comes on you; and you will be my witnesses in Jerusalem, and in all Judea and Samaria, and to the ends of the earth" (Acts 1:8).

Key Idea: God created a community through the nation of Israel to reveal his plan and point all people to the first coming of Jesus. Now God creates a new community called "the church" to reveal his plan and to point all people to the second coming of Christ. Believers form the body of Christ and collectively extend Jesus' presence and purpose earth.

God, the Spirit, who in the Old Testament previously existed behind the thick curtain in the temple, now takes up residence in believers in Christ, who represent his new temple.

GROUP DISCUSSION

Take a few minutes with your group members to discuss what you just watched and explore these concepts in Scripture.

1. What part of this week's teaching encouraged or challenged you the most? Why?

2. What was Jesus' instructions to the 120 believers in the upper room?

3. What were the believers to do when they received power from the Holy Spirit?

_____

_____

_____

_____

4. What happened after Peter delivered his message to the Jerusalem crowd?

_____

_____

_____

_____

5. What was unique about the way the members of the early church treated each other?

_____

_____

_____

_____

6. What is your biggest takeaway as you reflect on what you learned this week?

_____

_____

_____

_____

CLOSING PRAYER

End your group time by sharing prayer requests, reviewing how God has answered past prayers, and praying for one another. Use the space below to record any requests and praises. Also, make sure to pray for people God might add to your group—especially your neighbors.

Name   Request/Praise

_____   _____

_____   _____

_____   _____

_____   _____

_____   _____

FOR NEXT WEEK

Next week, we will look at the story of Paul's missionary journeys and how God expanded the church beyond Israel. Before your next group meeting, be sure to read through the following personal study, complete the exercises, and memorize the key verse for the session.

VIDEO NOTES ANSWER KEY

acknowledge, good news / kingdom, mission / witnesses, be / Holy Spirit, boldness / meal, remembering / salvation, new community

PERSONAL STUDY

Take some time after your group meeting this week to read through this section and complete the personal study. In total, it should take about one hour to complete. Allow the Scripture to take root in your heart as you review the story of the foundation of the early church.

KNOW THE STORY

Shortly before Jesus ascends into heaven, he gives instructions to his followers to take the message of God's salvation to the world. He stresses that this good news is for *everyone*, not just the Jewish people who had a head start because they worshiped the one true God. He instructs them to start in Jerusalem and then move out to Judea. From there they will go out into the next region, and then just keep going until everyone on the planet has heard the good news. As far as they were concerned, it all rested on them. But soon they would find this was not the case. They would have a supernatural Helper to assist them in fulfilling this calling.

> *In my former book, Theophilus, I wrote about all that Jesus began to do and to teach until the day he was taken up to heaven, after giving instructions through the Holy Spirit to the apostles he had chosen. After his suffering, he presented himself to them and gave many convincing proofs that he*

was alive. He appeared to them over a period of forty days and spoke about the kingdom of God. On one occasion, while he was eating with them, he gave them this command: "Do not leave Jerusalem, but wait for the gift my Father promised, which you have heard me speak about. For John baptized with water, but in a few days you will be baptized with the Holy Spirit."

Then they gathered around him and asked him, "Lord, are you at this time going to restore the kingdom to Israel?"

He said to them: "It is not for you to know the times or dates the Father has set by his own authority. But you will receive power when the Holy Spirit comes on you; and you will be my witnesses in Jerusalem, and in all Judea and Samaria, and to the ends of the earth."

After he said this, he was taken up before their very eyes, and a cloud hid him from their sight.

They were looking intently up into the sky as he was going, when suddenly two men dressed in white stood beside them. "Men of Galilee," they said, "why do you stand here looking into the sky? This same Jesus, who has been taken from you into heaven, will come back in the same way you have seen him go into heaven" (Acts 1:1–11).

When the day of Pentecost came, they were all together in one place. Suddenly a sound like the blowing of a violent wind came from heaven and filled the whole house where they were sitting. They saw what seemed to be tongues of fire that separated and came to rest on each of them. All of them were filled with the Holy Spirit and began to speak in other tongues as the Spirit enabled them.

Now there were staying in Jerusalem God-fearing Jews from every nation under heaven. When they heard this sound, a crowd came together in bewilderment, because each one heard their own language being spoken. Utterly amazed, they asked: "Aren't all these who are speaking Galileans? Then how is it that each of us hears them in our native language? Parthians, Medes and Elamites; residents of Mesopotamia, Judea and Cappadocia, Pontus and Asia, Phrygia and Pamphylia, Egypt and the parts of Libya near Cyrene; visitors from Rome (both Jews and converts to Judaism); Cretans and Arabs—we hear them declaring the wonders of God in our own tongues!" Amazed and perplexed, they asked one another, "What does this mean?"

Some, however, made fun of them and said, "They have had too much wine" (Acts 2:1–13).

Then Peter stood up with the Eleven, raised his voice and addressed the crowd: "Fellow Jews and all of you who live in Jerusalem, let me explain this to you; listen carefully to what I say. These people are not drunk, as you suppose. It's only nine in the morning! No, this is what was spoken by the prophet Joel:

> *"'In the last days, God says,*
>   *I will pour out my Spirit on all people.*
> *Your sons and daughters will prophesy,*
>   *your young men will see visions,*
>   *your old men will dream dreams.*
> *Even on my servants, both men and women,*
>   *I will pour out my Spirit in those days,*

and they will prophesy.
I will show wonders in the heavens above
    and signs on the earth below,
    blood and fire and billows of smoke.
The sun will be turned to darkness
    and the moon to blood
    before the coming of the great and glorious day
        of the Lord.
And everyone who calls
    on the name of the Lord will be saved.'

"Fellow Israelites, listen to this: Jesus of Nazareth was a man accredited by God to you by miracles, wonders and signs, which God did among you through him, as you your-selves know. This man was handed over to you by God's deliberate plan and foreknowledge; and you, with the help of wicked men, put him to death by nailing him to the cross. But God raised him from the dead, freeing him from the agony of death, because it was impossible for death to keep its hold on him. . . ."

"God has raised this Jesus to life, and we are all witnesses of it. Exalted to the right hand of God, he has received from the Father the promised Holy Spirit and has poured out what you now see and hear" (Acts 2:14–24, 32–33).

When the people heard this, they were cut to the heart and said to Peter and the other apostles, "Brothers, what shall we do?"

Peter replied, "Repent and be baptized, every one of you, in the name of Jesus Christ for the forgiveness of your sins. And you will receive the gift of the Holy Spirit. The promise is for you and your children and for all who are far off—for all whom the Lord our God will call."

With many other words he warned them; and he pleaded with them, "Save yourselves from this corrupt generation." Those who accepted his message were baptized, and about three thousand were added to their number that day.

They devoted themselves to the apostles' teaching and to fellowship, to the breaking of bread and to prayer. Everyone was filled with awe at the many wonders and signs performed by the apostles. All the believers were together and had everything in common. They sold property and possessions to give to anyone who had need. Every day they continued to meet together in the temple courts. They broke bread in their homes and ate together with glad and sincere hearts, praising God and enjoying the favor of all the people. And the Lord added to their number daily those who were being saved (Acts 2:37–47).

All the believers were one in heart and mind. No one claimed that any of their possessions was their own, but they shared everything they had. With great power the apostles continued to testify to the resurrection of the Lord Jesus. And God's grace was so powerfully at work in them all that there were no needy persons among them. For from time to time those who owned land or houses sold them, brought the money from the sales and put it at the apostles' feet, and it was distributed to anyone who had need.

Joseph, a Levite from Cyprus, whom the apostles called Barnabas (which means "son of encouragement"), sold a field he owned and brought the money and put it at the apostles' feet (Acts 4:32–37).

1. How did Jesus describe what his followers would receive if they waited in Jerusalem?

   _____

   _____

   _____

   _____

   _____

2. What events accompanied the coming of the Holy Spirit on the Day of Pentecost?

   _____

   _____

   _____

   _____

3. Why did Peter quote the prophecy from Joel to the people?

   _____

   _____

   _____

   _____

   _____

4. What did Peter say the people needed to do in response to his message?

   _____

   _____

   _____

   _____

5. What did certain members of the early church do to provide for the needs of others?

———— **UNDERSTAND THE STORY** ————

The followers of Jesus obeyed his instructions and waited in Jerusalem. Day after day they waited . . . and then it happened. Jerusalem was once again packed with people who had come to celebrate the holiday of Pentecost, which occurred fifty days after Passover. Suddenly, the Holy Spirit comes on them in the upper room like fire spreading on dry tinder. Immediately they are filled with a newfound courage and boldness to proclaim the message of the gospel.

Why did the Holy Spirit appear to them like "tongues of fire" (Acts 2:3)? One clue can be found by looking at how the Lord appeared to his people throughout the Story. God met Moses in the desert in the form of a burning bush. He led the Israelites in the form of a pillar of fire by night that guided them through their travels. He described himself as "a consuming fire" (Deuteronomy 4:24). Later, Elijah would call down "God's fire" from heaven to ignite a water-soaked altar to prove the Lord was superior to any others gods. The Lord would appear to Elijah in the form of a chariot of fire and take the prophet up to heaven in a whirlwind.

So it is no surprise that fire once again appeared on the day of Pentecost when the Holy Spirit fell on the believers who had gathered together. This time, however, he did not simply come upon them for a specific job, as he did the judges in the Old Testament. He filled them and *remained* with them. The people of God had become God's holy temple, replacing the man-made temple of stones and bricks. The opening chapters of the book of Acts give us a picture of what it looks like when God comes to live with—and in—human beings.

1. What do the stories you have read this week reveal about the power of the Holy Spirit?

   _____

   _____

   _____

   _____

   _____

   _____

2. How will these stories help you to better understand the impact of the Holy Spirit in your life as a believer and in your church community?

   _____

   _____

   _____

   _____

   _____

   _____

   _____

LIVE THE STORY

This part of the Story is so exciting because it is where our lives intersect with God in the upper story. Those of us who have accepted the gift of salvation have not only have been forgiven but have also received the Holy Spirit to empower us to live this new and better life. We have become a part of the church—the new community that God has established. Now, it is our job to be witnesses to the wonderful news of salvation. This certainly includes telling others about Jesus, but it is also expressed in how we treat others and live out the values of God's perfect community. This might be easy to do on a Sunday morning, but it's a lot harder to put into action during the week, when the lower story realities of life crowd out our upper story intentions. This is why we need the power of the Holy Spirit—to give us the courage and guidance we need to accomplish this task. The force of our message will be our changed lives.

1. How does a connection to the body of Christ, the church, help you be a solid witness for what God has done through Jesus' death and resurrection?

2. What is one action you will take this week to put what you've learned into practice?

_____

_____

_____

_____

_____

_____

_____

TELL THE STORY

One day this week around a meal or your dinner table, have a conversation about the topic of this session with family or friends. During your time together, read John 14:15–31, and then use the following question for discussion:

> *What do you think the Holy Spirit wants to do in our lives each day?*

Ask God this week to help you fully embrace the story of the rapid expansion of the early church. Also, spend a few minutes each day committing the key verse to memory: "But you will receive power when the Holy Spirit comes on you; and you will be my witnesses in Jerusalem, and in all Judea and Samaria, and to the ends of the earth" (Acts 1:8).

PAUL'S MISSION

ACTS 13–18

--- **WELCOME** ---

As followers of Christ, we all have a "conversion story"—a moment when we personally encountered the grace of God and decided to make Jesus the Lord of our lives. These conversion stories are as unique as our individual fingerprints. Some of us have a difficult time identifying a specific time when we first believed because we grew up in church. Others of us can point to a dramatic event— a serious illness, a tragic accident, the loss of a relationship—that woke us up to God's invitation. But few people have a conversion story as dramatic as the apostle Paul. On one of his missions to track down and exterminate the followers of Jesus, he came face-to-face with the risen Christ. What came out of that encounter not only changed Paul's life forever . . . but also changed the course of human history.

VIDEO TEACHING NOTES

Welcome to session six of *God the Savior*. Spend a few minutes sharing any insights or questions about last week's personal study. Then watch the video (see the streaming video access provided on the inside front cover). The answer key is found at the end of the session.

- The character in this session will experience more difficult _____ than rerouted airplanes and broken-down cars. He will be beaten, thrown into prison, and eventually beheaded for the _____ to his line of work.

- God calls Paul to finish out the _____ of Jesus to take the message of salvation to the "ends of the earth," where mostly the Gentiles lived. This is not only the _____ that Jesus gave the church but is also part of the promise that God made to Abraham some 2,100 years earlier.

- Paul connects the dots for people, relating how everything that happened to Jesus was _____ in the Old Testament—including everything that was done to him on the cross. Then he connects the dots to what is happening now. He goes for the close by offering up _____ to anyone who will believe.

- The Gentiles don't have the same _____ as the Jewish people. They don't know the stories of the Old Testament. They don't have a regard for Abraham and Moses. They don't worship Yahweh and aren't looking for a Messiah. Paul will need to _____ —and _____ he does!

- Paul's message radically changed people's lives in every city he visited. This challenged the _____ _____, which made people uptight. People stopped attending worship at the synagogues and pagan temples and started attending a little _____ church that Paul helped start.

- The upper story call on Paul's life was to take the gospel to the distant _____ of the earth. By God's grace, he did just that. He planted churches in highly Gentile populated cities. He also wrote thirteen _____ that helped strengthen the church, which are contained in our Bibles today.

GETTING STARTED

Begin your discussion by reciting the following key verses and key idea together as a group. Now try to state the key verses from memory. On your first attempt, use your notes if you need help. On your second attempt, try to state it completely from memory.

Key Verses: "Therefore, my friends, I want you to know that through Jesus the forgiveness of sins is proclaimed to you. Through him everyone who believes is set free from every sin, a justification you were not able to obtain under the law of Moses" (Acts 13:38–39).

Key Idea: God had told Abraham that all peoples on earth would be blessed through him, and now it was time to make good on that promise. God selects Paul to be the primary catalyst and directs him to take the message of Jesus to the Gentiles (everyone other than the Jews). Paul responds to that call and is responsible for planting many Gentile churches, strengthening numerous others, and writing thirteen of the twenty-seven books of the New Testament.

GROUP DISCUSSION

Take a few minutes with your group members to discuss what you just watched and explore these concepts in Scripture.

1. What part of this week's teaching encouraged or challenged you the most? Why?

2. What was Paul's role in God's plan of bringing the gospel to the world?

3. What was Paul's pattern for sharing the gospel when he arrived in a new city?

_____

_____

_____

_____

4. Why did Paul have to alter the way he presented the gospel to the Gentiles?

_____

_____

_____

_____

5. What radical changes occurred in the cities where Paul brought the gospel?

_____

_____

_____

_____

6. What is your biggest takeaway as you reflect on what you learned this week?

_____

_____

_____

_____

——— CLOSING PRAYER ———

End your group time by sharing prayer requests, reviewing how God has answered past prayers, and praying for one another. Use the space below to record any requests and praises. Also, make sure to pray for people God might add to your group—especially your neighbors.

Name   Request/Praise

_____   _____

_____   _____

_____   _____

_____   _____

_____   _____

——— FOR NEXT WEEK ———

Next week, we will look at the story of Paul's final days and how God worked mightily through him to the end of his life. Before your next group meeting, be sure to read through the following personal study, complete the exercises, and memorize the key verses for the session.

VIDEO NOTES ANSWER KEY

challenges, commitment / commission, commission / foretold, salvation / background, adjust, adjust / status quo, house / ends, letters

PERSONAL STUDY

Take some time after your group meeting this week to read through this section and complete the personal study. In total, it should take about one hour to complete. Allow the Scripture to take root in your heart as you review the story of Paul spreading the gospel to the world.

KNOW THE STORY

It is interesting to consider why God chose someone like Paul. As a self-proclaimed "Pharisee of Pharisees," he was trained in the nuances of Jewish religious life and seems an unlikely candidate to advocate the bringing of Gentiles into full inclusion in the covenant community—without the mark of circumcision, without observing the law, and without adopting Jewish rituals. But God chose to use this "Jew of Jews" to expand his family to the nations of the world. As the events of Acts unfold, we quickly see that Paul not only possessed a brilliant theological mind but also had an evangelist's zeal and a pastor's heart. He kept a near-frenetic pace, traveling throughout the Mediterranean world preaching, writing letters, and forming disciples.

Meanwhile, Saul was still breathing out murderous threats against the Lord's disciples. He went to the high priest and asked him for letters to the synagogues in Damascus, so that if he found any there who belonged to the Way, whether men or women, he might take them as prisoners to Jerusalem. As he neared Damascus on his journey, suddenly a light from heaven flashed around him. He fell to the ground and heard a voice say to him, "Saul, Saul, why do you persecute me?"

"Who are you, Lord?" Saul asked.

"I am Jesus, whom you are persecuting," he replied. "Now get up and go into the city, and you will be told what you must do."

The men traveling with Saul stood there speechless; they heard the sound but did not see anyone. Saul got up from the ground, but when he opened his eyes he could see nothing. So they led him by the hand into Damascus. For three days he was blind, and did not eat or drink anything.

In Damascus there was a disciple named Ananias. The Lord called to him in a vision, "Ananias!"

"Yes, Lord," he answered.

The Lord told him, "Go to the house of Judas on Straight Street and ask for a man from Tarsus named Saul, for he is praying. In a vision he has seen a man named Ananias come and place his hands on him to restore his sight."

"Lord," Ananias answered, "I have heard many reports about this man and all the harm he has done to your holy people in Jerusalem. And he has come here with authority from the chief priests to arrest all who call on your name."

But the Lord said to Ananias, "Go! This man is my chosen instrument to proclaim my name to the Gentiles and their kings and to the people of Israel. I will show him how much he must suffer for my name."

Then Ananias went to the house and entered it. Placing his hands on Saul, he said, "Brother Saul, the Lord—Jesus, who appeared to you on the road as you were coming here—has sent me so that you may see again and be filled with the Holy Spirit." Immediately, something like scales fell from Saul's eyes, and he could see again. He got up and was baptized, and after taking some food, he regained his strength.

Saul spent several days with the disciples in Damascus. At once he began to preach in the synagogues that Jesus is the Son of God. All those who heard him were astonished and asked, "Isn't he the man who raised havoc in Jerusalem among those who call on this name? And hasn't he come here to take them as prisoners to the chief priests?" Yet Saul grew more and more powerful and baffled the Jews living in Damascus by proving that Jesus is the Messiah (Acts 9:1–22).

Now those who had been scattered by the persecution that broke out when Stephen was killed traveled as far as Phoenicia, Cyprus and Antioch, spreading the word only among Jews. Some of them, however, men from Cyprus and Cyrene, went to Antioch and began to speak to Greeks also, telling them the good news about the Lord Jesus. The Lord's hand was with them, and a great number of people believed and turned to the Lord.

News of this reached the church in Jerusalem, and they sent Barnabas to Antioch. When he arrived and saw what the grace of God had done, he was glad and encouraged them all to remain true to the Lord with all their hearts. He was a good man, full of the Holy Spirit and faith, and a great number of people were brought to the Lord.

Then Barnabas went to Tarsus to look for Saul, and when he found him, he brought him to Antioch. So for a whole year Barnabas and Saul met with the church and taught great numbers of people. The disciples were called Christians first at Antioch.

During this time some prophets came down from Jerusalem to Antioch. One of them, named Agabus, stood up and through the Spirit predicted that a severe famine would spread over the entire Roman world. (This happened during the reign of Claudius.) The disciples, as each one was able, decided to provide help for the brothers and sisters living in Judea. This they did, sending their gift to the elders by Barnabas and Saul (Acts 11:19–30).

From Paphos, Paul and his companions sailed to Perga in Pamphylia, where John left them to return to Jerusalem. From Perga they went on to Pisidian Antioch. On the Sabbath they entered the synagogue and sat down. After the reading from the Law and the Prophets, the leaders of the synagogue sent word to them, saying, "Brothers, if you have a word of exhortation for the people, please speak."

Standing up, Paul motioned with his hand and said: "Fellow Israelites and you Gentiles who worship God, listen to me! . . . Fellow children of Abraham and you God-fearing Gentiles, it is to us that this message of salvation has been sent. The people of Jerusalem and their rulers did not recognize Jesus, yet in condemning him they fulfilled the words of the prophets that are read every Sabbath. Though they found no proper ground for a death sentence, they asked Pilate to have him executed. When they had carried out all that was written about him, they took him down from the cross and laid him in a tomb. But God raised him from the dead, and for many days he was seen by those who had traveled with him from Galilee to Jerusalem. They are now his witnesses to our people.

"We tell you the good news: What God promised our ancestors he has fulfilled for us, their children, by raising up Jesus. . . . Therefore, my friends, I want you to know that through Jesus the forgiveness of sins is proclaimed to you. Through him everyone who believes is set free from every sin, a justification you were not able to obtain under the law of Moses. . . ."

As Paul and Barnabas were leaving the synagogue, the people invited them to speak further about these things on the next Sabbath. When the congregation was dismissed, many of the Jews and devout converts to Judaism followed Paul and Barnabas, who talked with them and urged them to continue in the grace of God.

On the next Sabbath almost the whole city gathered to hear the word of the Lord. When the Jews saw the crowds, they were filled with jealousy. They began to contradict what Paul was saying and heaped abuse on him.

Then Paul and Barnabas answered them boldly: "We had to speak the word of God to you first. Since you reject it and do not consider yourselves worthy of eternal life, we now turn to the Gentiles" (Acts 13:13–16, 26–39, 42–46).

While Paul was waiting for them in Athens, he was greatly distressed to see that the city was full of idols. So he reasoned in the synagogue with both Jews and God-fearing Greeks, as well as in the marketplace day by day with those who happened to be there. A group of Epicurean and Stoic philosophers began to debate with him. Some of them asked, "What is this babbler trying to say?" Others remarked, "He seems to be advocating foreign gods." . . .

Paul then stood up in the meeting of the Areopagus and said: "People of Athens! I see that in every way you are very religious. For as I walked around and looked carefully at your objects of worship, I even found an altar with this inscription: TO AN UNKNOWN GOD. So you are ignorant of the very thing you worship—and this is what I am going to proclaim to you.

"The God who made the world and everything in it is the Lord of heaven and earth and does not live in temples built by human hands. And he is not served by human hands, as if he needed anything. Rather, he himself gives everyone life and breath and everything else. From one man he made all the nations, that they should inhabit the whole earth; and he marked out their appointed times in history and the boundaries of their lands. God did this so that they would seek him and perhaps reach out for him and find him, though he is not far from any one of us. 'For in him we live and move and have our being.' As some of your own poets have said, 'We are his offspring.'

"Therefore since we are God's offspring, we should not think that the divine being is like gold or silver or stone—an image made by human design and skill. In the past God overlooked such ignorance, but now he commands all people everywhere to repent. For he has set a day when he will judge the world with justice by the man he has appointed. He has given proof of this to everyone by raising him from the dead" (Acts 17:16–18, 22–31).

God did extraordinary miracles through Paul, so that even handkerchiefs and aprons that had touched him were taken to the sick, and their illnesses were cured and the evil spirits left them.

Some Jews who went around driving out evil spirits tried to invoke the name of the Lord Jesus over those who were demon-possessed. They would say, "In the name of the

Jesus whom Paul preaches, I command you to come out."
Seven sons of Sceva, a Jewish chief priest, were doing this.
One day the evil spirit answered them, "Jesus I know, and
Paul I know about, but who are you?" Then the man who
had the evil spirit jumped on them and overpowered them
all. He gave them such a beating that they ran out of the
house naked and bleeding.

When this became known to the Jews and Greeks living
in Ephesus, they were all seized with fear, and the name of
the Lord Jesus was held in high honor. Many of those who
believed now came and openly confessed what they had done.
A number who had practiced sorcery brought their scrolls
together and burned them publicly. When they calculated the
value of the scrolls, the total came to fifty thousand drach-
mas. In this way the word of the Lord spread widely and grew
in power (Acts 19:11–20).

1. How did God get Paul's attention when he was on the
   road to Damascus?

   _____

   _____

   _____

   _____

2. What did Barnabas do when he arrived in Antioch?

   _____

   _____

   _____

   _____

3. What "good news" did Paul proclaim to the Jews in Pisidian Antioch?

_____

_____

_____

_____

4. What did Paul proclaim about Jesus to the people in the city of Athens?

_____

_____

_____

_____

5. What extraordinary miracles took place as a result of Paul's ministry?

_____

_____

_____

_____

UNDERSTAND THE STORY

The early church grew by balancing two critical practices. The first was a radical dependence on the Holy Spirit to lead them and guide them in their mission. We see this in the early church's decision to commission Paul for his first missionary journey, which grew out of a concentrated season of prayer with several prophets and teachers in the church at Antioch.

The second practice of the early church was a strategic focus on key cultural centers. It is clear that Paul went to places where he could find potential leaders to carry the message forward. It was not an accident that he spread the message in the cities of the Roman world. Paul knew that these were the places where he would find the culture-shapers and communicators who could be discipled and sent out on mission. We also see that Paul had an intentional process that he followed in each city he visited. Paul started his work by seeking those who already exhibited faith in God, heading first to the synagogues.

It was during Paul's second missionary journey that he pushed farther toward Rome. Leaving the cities of Asia Minor, Paul headed into Macedonia and Greece, visiting some of the most influential urban centers of his day. On this mission trip, Paul also met a young man named Timothy and invited him to join him, assisting him in his missionary work. Timothy would become like a son to Paul and turn out to be a significant leader in the early church.

1. What do the stories you have read this week reveal about the calling and cost of sharing the gospel with others?

_____

_____

_____

_____

_____

_____

2. How will these stories help you better understand your need for godly friends who will encourage you to fulfill the plans God has for your life?

_____

_____

_____

_____

LIVE THE STORY

Paul's story reveals that God can use *anyone* to accomplish his plans. Paul was a prominent persecutor of Christians before he met Jesus on the road to Damascus, yet God chose him to be his ambassador and bring light to the world. Even before Paul met Jesus, God was preparing him by giving him the knowledge of Scripture and the tenacity of character that he would need for his mission. God will use our stories to advance his story as well—protagonists and antagonists alike. The difference is that those who are willing to align their lives with God's upper story receive the blessings that come from working alongside God in this mission.

1. How do you want God to use your story to share Jesus with the world?

_____

_____

_____

_____

2. What is one action you will take this week to put what you've learned into practice?

_____

_____

_____

_____

_____

_____

_____

_____

TELL THE STORY

One day this week around a meal or your dinner table, have a conversation about the topic of this session with family or friends. During your time together, read 1 Corinthians 1:4–9, and then use the following question for discussion:

What do you think that God has done to "enrich" us in every way?

Ask God this week to help you fully embrace the story of Paul's missionary journeys. Also, spend a few minutes each day committing the key verses to memory: "Therefore, my friends, I want you to know that through Jesus the forgiveness of sins is proclaimed to you. Through him everyone who believes is set free from every sin, a justification you were not able to obtain under the law of Moses" (Acts 13:38–39).

PAUL'S FINAL DAYS

ACTS 19–28

WELCOME

The apostle Paul loved to minister in the churches that he had helped to start. He enjoyed sharing the message of Christ, being a part of the local church, and watching followers of Jesus grow in their faith. But Paul could not be everywhere at the same time—and there were a *lot* of people in those churches who needed his guidance. So, Paul wrote *letters* to the new believers he left behind to help them understand how God wanted them to live. Paul wrote these letters from a number of different places, for a variety of different reasons, and under many different circumstances. As we will see in this session, Paul even wrote letters to churches and specific individuals when he was under Roman arrest—what we today know as the "Prison Epistles."

VIDEO TEACHING NOTES

Welcome to session seven of *God the Savior*. Spend a few minutes sharing any insights or questions about last week's personal study. Then watch the video (see the streaming video access provided on the inside front cover). The answer key is found at the end of the session.

- The only apostle who was not _____ for his faith is John. Paul, for his part, finds himself under house arrest in Rome. There he writes four letters we now appropriately call the _____ _____.

- Paul says that we are the body of Christ. We are to come together as one _____ community—one body, one Spirit, one hope, one Lord, one faith, one baptism, one God and Father of all. We are to use our _____ like different parts of the body to accomplish God's upper story purposes.

- Paul knows it is time to pass the baton to the next generation. One such student is a young man named _____. Paul built into him like a son. _____ is still young and is now on his own serving the church of Ephesus.

- It must have been challenging for Timothy to step out of his _____ _____ and lead in the midst of some _____ church folks who were looking down on him.

- If Timothy was released from prison, it meant he had gone to prison. If he went to prison, it means he had to _____ for his faith. God had raised up the next generation to carry the torch of Christ's great love with great _____.

- We need to be like Timothy. We need to fan into _____ the gift that God has given us—whatever that gift may be. We need to use it not toward our own selfish ends but to aid others in their _____ toward God.

GETTING STARTED

Begin your discussion by reciting the following key verses and key idea together as a group. Now try to state the key verses from memory. On your first attempt, use your notes if you need help. On your second attempt, try to state it completely from memory.

> **Key Verses:** "Follow God's example, therefore, as dearly loved children and walk in the way of love, just as Christ loved us and gave himself up for us as a fragrant offering and sacrifice to God" (Ephesians 5:1–2).

> **Key Idea:** The churches that Paul helped to establish are now in full motion, achieving the next chapter in God's grand story of redemption. Paul reminds believers in Christ that they are now part of a unified *body* and that each member has a specific part,

purpose, and function to perform. Paul knows that his time on earth is short, so he calls on co-workers like Timothy and Titus to continue this mission of spreading the gospel to the ends of the earth.

GROUP DISCUSSION

Take a few minutes with your group members to discuss what you just watched and explore these concepts in Scripture.

1. What part of this week's teaching encouraged or challenged you the most? Why?

2. How was Paul able to write a message of joy even from a prison cell?

3. Why was unity among believers so important to Paul?

4. How did Paul encourage the younger Timothy in his ministry?

5. What do you view as your role in the church—the body of Christ?

6. What is your biggest takeaway as you reflect on what you learned this week?

CLOSING PRAYER

End your group time by sharing prayer requests, reviewing how God has answered past prayers, and praying for one another. Use the space below to record any requests and praises. Also, make sure to pray for people God might add to your group—especially your neighbors.

Name   Request/Praise

_____   _____

_____   _____

_____   _____

_____   _____

FOR NEXT WEEK

Next week, we will look at the final words of John through the revelation and how those words bring the upper story full circle. Before your next group meeting, be sure to read through the following personal study, complete the exercises, and memorize the key verses for the session.

VIDEO NOTES ANSWER KEY

martyred, Prison Epistles / unified, gifts / Timothy, Timothy / comfort zone, older / stand up, boldness / flame, journey

PERSONAL STUDY

Take some time after your group meeting this week to read through this section and complete the personal study. In total, it should take about one hour to complete. Allow the Scripture to take root in your heart as you review the story of Paul's imprisonment and final days.

KNOW THE STORY

We were first introduced to Paul at the killing of Stephen, the first Christian martyr. At the end of Paul's life, the tables turn, and he is martyred for his unswerving and courageous faith. In his swan song, contained in his second letter to Timothy, he concludes that his life told a good story. He passes on this promise to us: "We know that in all things God works for the good of those who love him, who have been called according to his purpose" (Romans 8:28). When we align with God's upper story, he promises to write a good story with our lives.

> *And so we came to Rome. The brothers and sisters there had heard that we were coming, and they traveled as far as the Forum of Appius and the Three Taverns to meet us. At the sight of these people Paul thanked God and was encouraged. When we got to Rome, Paul was allowed to live by himself, with a soldier to guard him.*

Three days later he called together the local Jewish leaders. When they had assembled, Paul said to them: "My brothers, although I have done nothing against our people or against the customs of our ancestors, I was arrested in Jerusalem and handed over to the Romans. They examined me and wanted to release me, because I was not guilty of any crime deserving death. The Jews objected, so I was compelled to make an appeal to Caesar. I certainly did not intend to bring any charge against my own people. For this reason I have asked to see you and talk with you. It is because of the hope of Israel that I am bound with this chain."

They replied, "We have not received any letters from Judea concerning you, and none of our people who have come from there has reported or said anything bad about you. But we want to hear what your views are, for we know that people everywhere are talking against this sect."

They arranged to meet Paul on a certain day, and came in even larger numbers to the place where he was staying. He witnessed to them from morning till evening, explaining about the kingdom of God, and from the Law of Moses and from the Prophets he tried to persuade them about Jesus. Some were convinced by what he said, but others would not believe. They disagreed among themselves and began to leave after Paul had made this final statement: "The Holy Spirit spoke the truth to your ancestors when he said through Isaiah the prophet:

"'Go to this people and say,
"You will be ever hearing but never understanding;
you will be ever seeing but never perceiving."
For this people's heart has become calloused;

they hardly hear with their ears,
and they have closed their eyes.
Otherwise they might see with their eyes,
hear with their ears,
understand with their hearts
and turn, and I would heal them.'

"*Therefore I want you to know that God's salvation has been sent to the Gentiles, and they will listen!*"

For two whole years Paul stayed there in his own rented house and welcomed all who came to see him. He proclaimed the kingdom of God and taught about the Lord Jesus Christ—with all boldness and without hindrance! (Acts 28:14–31).

I rejoiced greatly in the Lord that at last you renewed your concern for me. Indeed, you were concerned, but you had no opportunity to show it. I am not saying this because I am in need, for I have learned to be content whatever the circumstances. I know what it is to be in need, and I know what it is to have plenty. I have learned the secret of being content in any and every situation, whether well fed or hungry, whether living in plenty or in want. I can do all this through him who gives me strength.

Yet it was good of you to share in my troubles. Moreover, as you Philippians know, in the early days of your acquaintance with the gospel, when I set out from Macedonia, not one church shared with me in the matter of giving and receiving, except you only; for even when I was in Thessalonica, you sent me aid more than once when I was in need. Not that I desire your gifts; what I desire is that more be credited to your account. I have received full payment and have more than enough. I am amply supplied, now that I have received from Epaphroditus the gifts you sent. They are a fragrant offering, an acceptable sacrifice, pleasing to God. And my God will meet all your needs according to the riches of his glory in Christ Jesus (Philippians 4:10–19).

As a prisoner for the Lord, then, I urge you to live a life worthy of the calling you have received. Be completely humble and gentle; be patient, bearing with one another in love. Make every effort to keep the unity of the Spirit through the bond of peace. There is one body and one Spirit, just as you were called to one hope when you were called; one Lord, one faith, one baptism; one God and Father of all, who is over all and through all and in all.

But to each one of us grace has been given as Christ apportioned it. This is why it says: "When he ascended on high, he took many captives and gave gifts to his people."

(What does "he ascended" mean except that he also descended to the lower, earthly regions? He who descended is the very one who ascended higher than all the heavens, in order to fill the whole universe.) So Christ himself gave the apostles, the prophets, the evangelists, the pastors and teachers, to equip his people for works of service, so that the body of Christ may be built up until we all reach unity in the faith and in the knowledge of the Son of God and become mature, attaining to the whole measure of the fullness of Christ.

Then we will no longer be infants, tossed back and forth by the waves, and blown here and there by every wind of teaching and by the cunning and craftiness of people in their deceitful scheming. Instead, speaking the truth in love, we will grow to become in every respect the mature body of him who is the head, that is, Christ. From him the whole body, joined and held together by every supporting ligament, grows and builds itself up in love, as each part does its work (Ephesians 4:1–16).

I thank God, whom I serve, as my ancestors did, with a clear conscience, as night and day I constantly remember you in my prayers. Recalling your tears, I long to see you, so that I may be filled with joy. I am reminded of your sincere faith, which first lived in your grandmother Lois and in your mother Eunice and, I am persuaded, now lives in you also.

For this reason I remind you to fan into flame the gift of God, which is in you through the laying on of my hands. For the Spirit God gave us does not make us timid, but gives us power, love and self-discipline. So do not be ashamed of the testimony about our Lord or of me his prisoner. Rather, join with me in suffering for the gospel, by the power of God. He has saved us and called us to a holy life—not because of anything we have done but because of his own purpose and grace. This grace was given us in Christ Jesus before the beginning of time, but it has now been revealed through the appearing of our Savior, Christ Jesus, who has destroyed death and has brought life and immortality to light through the gospel. And of this gospel I was appointed a herald and an apostle and a teacher. That is why I am suffering as I am. Yet this is no cause for shame, because I know whom I have believed, and am convinced that he is able to guard what I have entrusted to him until that day.

What you heard from me, keep as the pattern of sound teaching, with faith and love in Christ Jesus. Guard the good deposit that was entrusted to you—guard it with the help of the Holy Spirit who lives in us (2 Timothy 1:3–14).

In the presence of God and of Christ Jesus, who will judge the living and the dead, and in view of his appearing and his kingdom, I give you this charge: Preach the word; be prepared in season and out of season; correct, rebuke and encourage—with great patience and careful instruction. For the time will come when people will not put up with sound doctrine. Instead, to suit their own desires, they will gather around them a great number of teachers to say what their itching ears want to hear. They will turn their ears away from the truth and turn aside to myths. But you, keep your head in all situations, endure hardship, do the work of an evangelist, discharge all the duties of your ministry.

For I am already being poured out like a drink offering, and the time for my departure is near. I have fought the good fight, I have finished the race, I have kept the faith. Now there is in store for me the crown of righteousness, which the Lord, the righteous Judge, will award to me on that day—and not only to me, but also to all who have longed for his appearing (2 Timothy 4:1–8).

1. What did the apostle Paul do after arriving in Rome under house arrest?

_____

_____

_____

_____

_____

_____

2. What caused Paul to rejoice when he considered the Philippians?

_____

_____

_____

3. What did Paul tell the Ephesians was the purpose of spiritual gifts?

_____

_____

_____

_____

4. How did Paul explain the reason for his suffering to Timothy?

_____

_____

_____

_____

5. What final charge did Paul give to Timothy?

_____

_____

_____

_____

UNDERSTAND THE STORY

As we have seen, Paul kept up a tiring schedule, constantly traveling. He was, without a doubt, a man of action. Yet Paul also had an incredible focus on building relationships. One of the clearest indicators of this comes when we read the end of each of his letters. In most of them, we find an extensive list of people he is praying for and thinking about. Each name in the letters represents a personal relationship that Paul has built. It is through these relationships—and the love and encouragement so evident in his letters—that disciples are made.

Paul's journeys eventually take him back to Jerusalem. Sadly, even though the city had once been his home, he was now an unwelcome guest because of his consistent preaching in the name of Jesus Christ, a condemned and executed "disturber of the peace." To add insult to injury, Paul had also committed a terrible crime: he had reached out to the *Gentiles*! Just as the religious leaders had done with Jesus, they soon were plotting to end Paul's life.

These efforts eventually led to Paul being imprisoned in Rome after a storm-ridden boat ride. Yet even from a confined jail cell, he still found moments to pen letters to his friends and to the churches he had planted. He encouraged them to grow in their faith, stand firm in the face of persecution, and focus on the gift of eternal life they had received through Christ. As they did these things, they would find they could handle anything that life threw at them.

1. What do the stories you have read this week tell you about how you can always remain joyful in Christ?

_____

_____

_____

_____

2. How will these stories help you when you are going through a trying time?

_____

_____

_____

LIVE THE STORY

Paul's story reveals that the way we lead our lives is often the most convincing message for Christ. From a lower story perspective, following Jesus can be risky. Like Paul, we will encounter twists and turns and bumps and bruises along the way. It is how we choose to respond to those challenges that will show whether we have truly been "chiseled" to look like Christ. Do we lean into the fear and fall into despair? Or do we place our faith in Jesus and look to him for strength? If we live like those who do not know Jesus, no one will want to become a part of God's community. But if we focus on Christ in spite of our trials, others will be drawn to the strength that they see in us. Our role is to let God chisel away anything in our lives that doesn't look like Jesus until others will be able to see him in us and decide to follow him as well.

1. What are some ways that God has "chiseled" you through circumstances?

_____

_____

_____

_____

2. What is one action you will take this week to put what you've learned into practice?

_____

_____

_____

_____

TELL THE STORY

One day this week around a meal or your dinner table, have a conversation about the topic of this session with family or friends. During your time together, read Romans 8:26–30, and then use the following question for discussion:

How does God help us when we experiences times of struggle and uncertainty?

Ask God this week to help you fully embrace the story of Paul's final days of ministry. Also, spend a few minutes each day committing the key verses to memory: "Follow God's example, therefore, as dearly loved children and walk in the way of love, just as Christ loved us and gave himself up for us as a fragrant offering and sacrifice to God" (Ephesians 5:1–2).

THE END OF TIME

REVELATION

WELCOME

Have you ever read a book or listened to a story that you didn't want to end? A story so good that you just wanted it to keep going and going? The final book of the Bible is appropriately called "Revelation" because it reveals how life on earth—our lower story—will come to an end. However, it could just as easily have been called "The New Beginning," because it is all about what life in God's perfect community will be like after the events in our world have come to a close. As we know, God's upper story will never end—it will just keep going on and on forever. So, as we will discuss in this final session, while Revelation may mark the end of the Bible, it is really just the beginning of a brand-new adventure for all followers of Jesus Christ.

VIDEO TEACHING NOTES

Welcome to session eight of *God the Savior*. Spend a few minutes sharing any insights or questions about last week's personal study. Then watch the video (see the streaming video access provided on the inside front cover). The answer key is found at the end of the session.

- We received the book of _____ from the disciple John. He is the same who wrote the Gospel of John and the letters of 1, 2, and 3 John. He was one of the original disciples of Jesus. He was known as the "_____" disciple.

- John's vision reveals that God will come down into the lower story to be with us like he was with _____ and _____. There is no mention of a tabernacle or a temple. There is no mention of a barrier or curtain between God and people or a room called the Holy of Holies. He is just _____ us.

- God will take that same finger he used in Michelangelo's painting to give life to Adam and wipe the final _____ from our eyes. There will be no more illness, no more hatred, no more fighting, no more selfishness, no more _____.

- God has reconstructed the _____. Here we find the Tree of Life again—the tree that bore fruit to eternal life. We now have unguarded access to it. And there's not just one tree. There are ____ Trees of Life that reside on either side of the great river that bear fruit not once a year but every month.

- Most important of all, in that place we will see God's _____. We will see the intense love in his eyes that went to such great extent to get us back. It will overwhelm us every day for _____ and will compel us to worship him.

- God's upper story vision has been completely _____. He will come down into our lower story and do life with us forever. If we are followers of Christ, no matter how difficult things become in this life, no matter how dark, we can take _____ because we know this is not how our story ends.

GETTING STARTED

Begin your discussion by reciting the following key verses and key idea together as a group. Now try to state the key verses from memory. On your first attempt, use your notes if you need help. On your second attempt, try to state them completely from memory.

Key Verses: "Then I saw 'a new heaven and a new earth,' for the first heaven and the first earth had passed away, and there was no longer any sea. I saw the Holy City, the new Jerusalem, coming down out of heaven from God, prepared as a bride beautifully dressed for her husband" (Revelation 21:1–2).

Key Idea: The last two chapters of the Bible read almost the same as the first two chapters in the Bible. God is creating a new heaven and a new earth. The tree of life is at the center of the garden. A community of people will be there with new bodies that are not infected with sin. The tree of the knowledge of good and evil that gave Adam and Eve the choice to reject God's vision is not there. God has come down to live among his people and take a walk with them in the "cool of the day." This is not really the ending of the story, but a new beginning. God has restored what was lost in the first beginning through Christ.

GROUP DISCUSSION

Take a few minutes with your group members to discuss what you just watched and explore these concepts in Scripture.

1. What part of this week's teaching encouraged or challenged you the most? Why?

2. What were the religious leaders hoping to accomplish by banishing John to Patmos?

3. How is the picture that John paints of the new heaven and the new earth *similar* to the one we are given in the book of Genesis?

4. What is *different* about this picture we are given of the new heaven and new earth?

5. Why is it important that there is no mention of the tree of knowledge of good and evil?

6. What is your biggest takeaway as you reflect on what you learned this week?

———— CLOSING PRAYER ————

End your group time by sharing prayer requests, reviewing how God has answered past prayers, and praying for one another. Use the space below to record any requests and praises. Also, make sure to pray for people God might add to your group—especially your neighbors.

Name   Request/Praise

_____   _____

_____   _____

_____   _____

_____   _____

_____   _____

_____   _____

_____   _____

_____   _____

———— IN THE COMING DAYS ————

In the days ahead, be sure to read through the following personal study, complete the exercises, and memorize the key verses for the session.

VIDEO NOTES ANSWER KEY

Revelation, beloved / Adam, Eve, with / tear, death / garden, two / face, eternity / restored, courage

PERSONAL STUDY

Take some time after your group meeting this week to read through this section and complete the personal study. In total, it should take about one hour to complete. Allow the Scripture to take root in your heart as you review the story of God's coming promises to his people.

KNOW THE STORY

The book of Revelation was penned by John, known as the "disciple whom Jesus loved." He is the one who was so excited about the news of the empty tomb that he outran Peter to be the first to arrive there. By the time he wrote this book, he probably couldn't run quite so fast anymore. Historians tell us that he is the only apostle who was not killed for professing his faith in Jesus Christ. Instead, he was banished to a bleak and remote island called Patmos. It is on this island that God visits the beloved John and gives him a clear vision of what is yet to come, including the best picture we have of what the kingdom of God is going to be like.

The revelation from Jesus Christ, which God gave him to show his servants what must soon take place. He made it known by sending his angel to his servant John, who testifies to everything he saw—that is, the word of God and the testimony of Jesus Christ. Blessed is the one who reads aloud the words of this prophecy, and blessed are those who hear it and take to heart what is written in it, because the time is near. . . .

I, John, your brother and companion in the suffering and kingdom and patient endurance that are ours in Jesus, was on the island of Patmos because of the word of God and the testimony of Jesus. On the Lord's Day I was in the Spirit, and I heard behind me a loud voice like a trumpet, which said: "Write on a scroll what you see and send it to the seven churches: to Ephesus, Smyrna, Pergamum, Thyatira, Sardis, Philadelphia and Laodicea."

I turned around to see the voice that was speaking to me. And when I turned I saw seven golden lampstands, and among the lampstands was someone like a son of man, dressed in a robe reaching down to his feet and with a golden sash around his chest. The hair on his head was white like wool, as white as snow, and his eyes were like blazing fire. His feet were like bronze glowing in a furnace, and his voice was like the sound of rushing waters. In his right hand he held seven stars, and coming out of his mouth was a sharp, double-edged sword. His face was like the sun shining in all its brilliance.

When I saw him, I fell at his feet as though dead. Then he placed his right hand on me and said: "Do not be afraid. I am the First and the Last. I am the Living One; I was dead, and now look, I am alive for ever and ever! And I hold the keys of death and Hades" (Revelation 1:1–3, 9–18).

Then I saw "a new heaven and a new earth," for the first heaven and the first earth had passed away, and there was no longer any sea. I saw the Holy City, the new Jerusalem, coming down out of heaven from God, prepared as a bride beautifully dressed for her husband. And I heard a loud voice from the throne saying, "Look! God's dwelling place is now among the people, and he will dwell with them. They will be his people, and God himself will be with them and be their God. 'He will wipe every tear from their eyes. There will be no more death' or mourning or crying or pain, for the old order of things has passed away."

He who was seated on the throne said, "I am making everything new!" Then he said, "Write this down, for these words are trustworthy and true."

He said to me: "It is done. I am the Alpha and the Omega, the Beginning and the End. To the thirsty I will give water without cost from the spring of the water of life. Those who are victorious will inherit all this, and I will be their God and they will be my children. But the cowardly, the unbelieving, the vile, the murderers, the sexually immoral, those who practice magic arts, the idolaters and all liars—they will be consigned to the fiery lake of burning sulfur. This is the second death" (Revelation 21:1-8).

One of the seven angels who had the seven bowls full of the seven last plagues came and said to me, "Come, I will show you the bride, the wife of the Lamb." And he carried me away in the Spirit to a mountain great and high, and showed me the Holy City, Jerusalem, coming down out of heaven from God. It shone with the glory of God, and its brilliance was like that of a very precious jewel, like a jasper, clear as crystal. It had a great, high wall with twelve gates, and with twelve angels at the gates. On the gates were written the names of the twelve tribes of Israel. There were three gates on the east, three on the north, three on the south and three on the west. The wall of the city had twelve foundations, and on them were the names of the twelve apostles of the Lamb.

The angel who talked with me had a measuring rod of gold to measure the city, its gates and its walls. The city was laid out like a square, as long as it was wide. He measured the city with the rod and found it to be 12,000 stadia in length, and as wide and high as it is long. The angel measured the wall using human measurement, and it was 144 cubits thick. The wall was made of jasper, and the city of pure gold, as pure as glass. The foundations of the city walls were decorated with every kind of precious stone. The first foundation was jasper, the second sapphire, the third agate, the fourth emerald, the fifth onyx, the sixth ruby, the seventh chrysolite, the eighth beryl, the ninth topaz, the tenth turquoise, the eleventh jacinth, and the twelfth amethyst. The twelve gates were twelve pearls, each gate made of a single pearl. The great street of the city was of gold, as pure as transparent glass.

I did not see a temple in the city, because the Lord God Almighty and the Lamb are its temple. The city does not need the sun or the moon to shine on it, for the glory of God gives it light, and the Lamb is its lamp. The nations will walk by its light, and the kings of the earth will bring their splendor into it. On no day will its gates ever be shut, for there will be no night there. The glory and honor of the nations will be brought into it. Nothing impure will ever enter it, nor will anyone who does what is shameful or deceitful, but only those whose names are written in the Lamb's book of life (Revelation 21:9–27).

Then the angel showed me the river of the water of life, as clear as crystal, flowing from the throne of God and of the

Lamb down the middle of the great street of the city. On each side of the river stood the tree of life, bearing twelve crops of fruit, yielding its fruit every month. And the leaves of the tree are for the healing of the nations. No longer will there be any curse. The throne of God and of the Lamb will be in the city, and his servants will serve him. They will see his face, and his name will be on their foreheads. There will be no more night. They will not need the light of a lamp or the light of the sun, for the Lord God will give them light. And they will reign for ever and ever.

The angel said to me, "These words are trustworthy and true. The Lord, the God who inspires the prophets, sent his angel to show his servants the things that must soon take place."

"Look, I am coming soon! Blessed is the one who keeps the words of the prophecy written in this scroll."

I, John, am the one who heard and saw these things. And when I had heard and seen them, I fell down to worship at the feet of the angel who had been showing them to me. But he said to me, "Don't do that! I am a fellow servant with you and with your fellow prophets and with all who keep the words of this scroll. Worship God!"

Then he told me, "Do not seal up the words of the prophecy of this scroll, because the time is near. Let the one who does wrong continue to do wrong; let the vile person continue to be vile; let the one who does right continue to do right; and let the holy person continue to be holy" (Revelation 22:1–11).

"Look, I am coming soon! My reward is with me, and I will give to each person according to what they have done. I am the Alpha and the Omega, the First and the Last, the Beginning and the End.

"Blessed are those who wash their robes, that they may have the right to the tree of life and may go through the gates into the city. Outside are the dogs, those who practice magic arts, the sexually immoral, the murderers, the idolaters and everyone who loves and practices falsehood.

"I, Jesus, have sent my angel to give you this testimony for the churches. I am the Root and the Offspring of David, and the bright Morning Star."

The Spirit and the bride say, "Come!" And let the one who hears say, "Come!" Let the one who is thirsty come; and let the one who wishes take the free gift of the water of life.

I warn everyone who hears the words of the prophecy of this scroll: If anyone adds anything to them, God will add to that person the plagues described in this scroll. And if anyone takes words away from this scroll of prophecy, God will take away from that person any share in the tree of life and in the Holy City, which are described in this scroll.

He who testifies to these things says, "Yes, I am coming soon."

Amen. Come, Lord Jesus.

The grace of the Lord Jesus be with God's people. Amen (Revelation 22:12–21).

1. How does John describe Jesus' appearance in his vision?

2. What does God say will be "no more" be in the new heaven and new earth?

_____

_____

_____

_____

3. What reason does John provide for their not being a temple in the New Jerusalem?

_____

_____

_____

_____

4. What details does John provide about the trees of life on each side of the river?

_____

_____

_____

_____

5. What blessings does Jesus promise to those who come to him?

_____

_____

_____

_____

UNDERSTAND THE STORY

The book of Revelation is often reduced to a strange blend between a complex crossword puzzle and a tricked-out tarot card. But the reality is that there are many clear, inspiring, stunning, and worship-inducing truths in the book of Revelation. John's vision accomplishes something more than simply showing us the *future* . . . it shows us the *center*. It shows us that the God who reigns on a throne, high and holy, is also the Lord who sent his one and only Son to die on a cross and rescue sinners. The Lamb who was slain is now alive forevermore. For all eternity we will see, savor, and celebrate the goodness and glory of the God who saves.

God's story doesn't make a line but a circle back to where all that has been broken is restored. In fact, the last two chapters in the book of Revelation read almost identically to the first two chapters of the book of Genesis. God is creating a *new* heaven and a *new* earth. The tree of *life* is there at the center of the garden. A community of people will be present with *new* bodies that are not infected with sin. The tree of the knowledge of good and evil that gave Adam and Eve the choice to reject God's vision is not to be found. God has come down to live among us and take a walk with us in the "cool of the day" just as he did in Eden.

God does not simply recreate a beautiful world that has been marred and stained by human sin. The story of our redemption, healing, and the new work of creation through Jesus Christ shows us something deeper about God. In response to our sin and rebellion, God is both just and gracious. In his righteous judgment against sin, he has graciously made a way for his people to behold him, know him, and love him. That is what we were made to do, and it is the hope of our future: to live with God forever in a world renewed and freed from the curse of sin.

1. What does the story you have read this week tell you about God's plan for the future?

   _____

   _____

   _____

   _____

2. How does this vision help you have hope and courage today?

   _____

   _____

   _____

   _____

LIVE THE STORY

The events in Revelation are still to come . . . which means that *you* are a character in God's story. You have a role to play! The same God who called and empowered ordinary people to do extraordinary things during Bible times is doing the same today. He is taking your lower story and writing it into his upper story. Through your life, others can discover the grace of God and become your neighbors in the new garden for all eternity. As you draw close to God, you will hear his instruction on what to do, and you will see his hand weaving the details of your life to move his story forward. Nothing will bring greater fulfillment than knowing you have a purpose in God. So live every day with the expectation that this could be the day your Savior returns.

1. How does the assurance of a beautiful future with God impact your desire to share your hope in Jesus with other people who need his grace?

_____

_____

_____

_____

_____

2. What is one action you will take this week to put what you've learned into practice?

_____

_____

_____

_____

TELL THE STORY

One day this week around a meal or your dinner table, have a conversation about the topic of this session with family or friends. During your time together, read Revelation 21:9–27, and then use the following question for discussion:

What goes through your mind when you think about spending eternity with God?

Ask God this week to help you fully embrace the story of God's future for his chosen people. Also, spend a few minutes each day committing the key verses to memory: "Then I saw 'a new heaven and a new earth,' for the first heaven and the first earth had passed away, and there was no longer any sea. I saw the Holy City, the new Jerusalem, coming down out of heaven from God, prepared as a bride beautifully dressed for her husband" (Revelation 21:1–2).

LEADER'S GUIDE

Thank you for your willingness to lead your group through this study! What you have chosen to do is valuable and will make a great difference in the lives of others. The rewards of being a leader are different from those participating, and we hope that as you lead you will find your own walk with Jesus deepened by this experience.

God the Savior is an eight-session study in *The Story* series built around video content and small-group interaction. As the group leader, just think of yourself as the host of a dinner party. Your job is to take care of your guests by managing all the behind-the-scenes details so that when everyone arrives, they can just enjoy time together.

As the group leader, your role is not to answer all the questions or reteach the content—the video and study guide will do most of that work. Your job is to guide the experience and cultivate your small group into a kind of teaching community. This will make it a place for members to process, question, and reflect—not receive more instruction.

Before your first meeting, make sure everyone in the group gets a copy of the study guide. This will keep everyone on the same page and help the process run more smoothly. If some group members are unable to purchase the guide, arrange it so that people can share the resource with other group members. Giving everyone access to all the material will position this study to be as rewarding an experience as possible. Everyone should feel free to write in his or her study guide and bring it to group every week.

SETTING UP THE GROUP

You will need to determine with your group how long you want to meet each week so that you can plan your time accordingly. Generally, most groups like to meet for either ninety minutes or two hours, so you could use one of the following schedules:

SECTION	90 MINUTES	120 MINUTES
WELCOME (members arrive and get settled)	15 minutes	15 minutes
WATCH (watch the teaching material together and take notes)	15 minutes	15 minutes
DISCUSS (recite the key verse and key idea and discuss study questions you selected)	40 minutes	60 minutes
PRAY (close your time in prayer)	20 minutes	30 minutes

As the group leader, you will want to create an environment that encourages sharing and learning. A church sanctuary or formal classroom may not be as ideal as a living room in this regard, because those locations can feel formal and less intimate. No matter what setting you choose, provide enough comfortable seating for everyone, and, if possible, arrange the seats in a semicircle so everyone can see the video easily. This will make transition between the video and group conversation more efficient and natural.

If you are meeting in person, get to the meeting site early so you can greet participants as they arrive. Simple refreshments create a welcoming atmosphere and can be a wonderful addition to a group study evening. Be sure to take food and pet allergies into account to make your guests as comfortable as possible. You may also want to consider offering childcare to couples with children who want to attend. Finally, be sure your media technology is working properly. Managing these details up front will make the rest of your group experience flow smoothly and provide a welcoming space to engage the content of *God the Savior.*

STRUCTURING THE GROUP TIME

Once everyone has arrived, it's time to begin the group. Here are some simple tips to make your group time healthy, enjoyable, and effective.

First, begin the meeting with a short prayer and remind the group members to put their phones on silent. This is a way to make sure you can all be present with one another and with God. Next, watch the video and instruct the participants to follow along in their guides and take notes. After the video teaching, have the group recite the key verse and key idea together before moving on to the discussion questions.

Encourage all the group members to participate in the discussion, but make sure they know they don't have to do so.

As the discussion progresses, you may want to follow up with comments such as, "Tell me more about that," or, "Why did you answer that way?" This will allow the group participants to deepen their reflections and invite meaningful sharing in a nonthreatening way.

Note that you have been given multiple questions to use in each session, and you do not have to use them all or even follow them in order. Feel free to pick and choose questions based on either the needs of your group or how the conversation is flowing. Also, don't be afraid of silence. Offering a question and allowing up to thirty seconds of silence is okay. It allows people space to think about how they want to respond and also gives them time to do so.

As group leader, you are the boundary keeper for your group. Do not let anyone (yourself included) dominate the group time. Keep an eye out for group members who might be tempted to "attack" folks they disagree with or try to "fix" those having struggles. These kinds of behaviors can derail a group's momentum, so they need to be steered in a different direction. Model active listening and encourage everyone in your group to do the same. This will make your group time a safe space and create a positive community.

CONCLUDING THE GROUP TIME

At the conclusion of session one, invite the group members to complete the between-sessions personal studies for that week. Also let them know that if they choose to do so, they can watch the video for the following week by accessing the streaming code found on the inside front cover of their studies. Explain that you will be providing some time before the video teaching the following week for anyone to share any insights. (Do this as part of the opening "Welcome" beginning in session two, right before you watch the video.) Let them know sharing is optional.

Thank you again for taking the time to lead your group and helping them to understand the greater story of the Bible in *God the Savior*. You are making a difference in the lives of others and having an impact for the kingdom of God!

God the Creator
Our Beginning, Our Rebellion, and Our Way Back

Study Guide
9780310135203

DVD with
Free Streaming Access
9780310135227

This study will introduce you to the lower and upper stories as told in the Old Testament books of Genesis through Ruth where we discover God's creation of the world and his plan of redemption of humankind. As you read these narratives—featuring characters such as Adam, Eve, Abraham, Sarah, Joseph, Moses, Joshua, Gideon, and Ruth—you will see how God has been weaving our lower story into the greater upper story that he has been writing.

God the Deliverer

Our Search for Identity and Our Hope for Renewal

Study Guide
9780310134787

DVD with
Free Streaming Access
9780310134800

This study will introduce you to the lower and upper stories as told in the Old Testament books of 1 Samuel through Malachi to explore how God's plan was at work through the exile and restoration of Israel. As you read these narratives—featuring characters such as Samuel, Saul, David, Jeremiah, Daniel, Esther, Ezra, and Nehemiah—you will see how God has been weaving our lower story into the greater upper story that he has been writing.

THE STORY

POWERED BY **ZONDERVAN®**

READ THE STORY. EXPERIENCE THE BIBLE.

Here I am, 50 years old. I have been to college, seminary, engaged in ministry my whole life, my dad is in ministry, my grandfather was in ministry, and **The Story has been one of the most unique experiences of my life**. The Bible has been made fresh for me. It has made God's redemptive plan come alive for me once again.
—Seth Buckley, Youth Pastor,
Spartanburg Baptist Church, Spartanburg, SC

As my family and I went through *The Story* together, the more I began to believe and the more real [the Bible] became to me, and **it rubbed off on my children and helped them with their walk with the Lord**. *The Story* inspired conversations we might not normally have had.
—Kelly Leonard, Parent, Shepherd of the Hills Christian Church, Porter Ranch, CA

We have people reading ***The Story*—some devour it and can't wait for the next week**. Some have never really read the Bible much, so it's exciting to see a lot of adults reading the Word of God for the first time. I've heard wonderful things from people who are long-time readers of Scripture. They're excited about how it's all being tied together for them. It just seems to make more sense.
—Lynnette Schulz,
Director of Worship
Peace Lutheran Church,
Eau Claire, WI

FOR ADULTS

9780310458197

FOR TEENS

9780310458463

FOR KIDS

9780310719250

TheStory.com

The Life-Changing
Bible Engagement Experience
That Will
Transform
Your Church

Impactful, proven, trusted, and easy to implement, THE STORY is the gold-standard Bible engagement program for whole churches.

THE STORY

With curriculum and books for all ages, along with preaching resources, small group study, youth group activities, and parent helps, *The Story Church Resource Kit* is your complete resource for the entire ministry year.

FOR CHILDREN

FOR CHURCHES

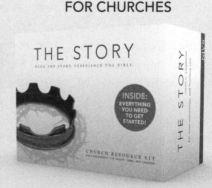

9780310719755   9780310719274   Campaign Kit   9780310941538

THE STORY
POWERED BY ZONDERVAN

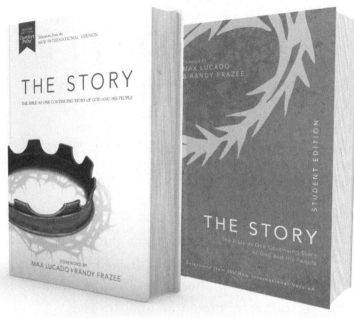

If You Want to Grow in Your Faith, You Must Engage God's Word

What you believe in your heart will define who you become. God wants you to become like Jesus—it is the most truthful and powerful way to live—and the journey to becoming like Jesus begins by thinking like Jesus.

Jesus compared the Christian life to a vine. He is the vine; you are the branches. If you remain in the vine of Christ, over time you will produce amazing and scrumptious fruit for all to see and taste. You begin to act like Jesus, and become more like Jesus.

In the **Believe Bible Study Series**, bestselling author and pastor Randy Frazee helps you ask three big questions:

- What do I believe and why does it matter?
- How can I put my faith into action?
- Am I becoming the person God wants me to be?

Each of the three eight-session studies in this series include video teaching from Randy Frazee and a study guide with video study notes, group discussion questions, Scripture reading, and activities for personal growth and reflection.

As you journey through this study series, whether in a group or on your own, one simple truth will become undeniably clear: what you believe drives everything.

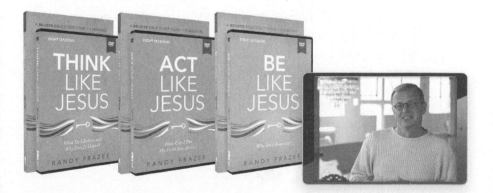

Available now at your favorite bookstore, or streaming video on StudyGateway.com.